Great British MotorCycles of the Sixties

Bob Currie

MOTOR CYCLE WEEKLY

HAMLYN London · New York · Sydney · Toronto

Contents

Published by The Hamlyn Publishing Group Limited
London · New York · Sydney · Toronto
Astronaut House, Feltham, Middlesex, England
© Copyright IPC Specialist & Professional Press Limited 1981
All rights reserved. No part of this publication may be reproduced,
stored in a retrieval system, or transmitted, in any form or by any
means, electronic, mechanical, photocopying, recording or otherwise,
without the permission of The Hamlyn Publishing Group Limited
and the copyrightholder.

ISBN 0 600 34980 2

Printed in Great Britain

Title pages: a 1962 Royal Enfield Super-5, ancestor of the
Continental GT, pauses by the Guthrie Memorial, alongside the
Isle of Man TT course

Introduction

That the 1960s saw the decline and virtual total eclipse of the once-proud British motor cycle industry is well enough known; what is really astonishing is that it should have taken place in such a short space of time. As the decade began, motor cycling was on the crest of a wave, with a total of 1,853,000 machines in use on the roads of Britain. Admittedly, that total included a proportion of Italian-made scooters, and German and French mopeds, but the bulk were certainly home-manufactured. Moreover, it did not take into account the many BSAs, Greeves, Dots, Cottons and Matchlesses, which were not registered for road use but kept solely for competition purposes.

Yet as 1969 drew to a close the tale was one of stark tragedy. The giant AMC group, embracing Matchless, AJS, Norton, James and Francis-Barnett had already gone to the wall, and though it is true that Norton and AJS had been salvaged by Dennis Poore and his new Norton-Villiers firm, production was at a rather lower level than before. Velocette were in deep trouble and would cease operations by 1970. Acquired by financial speculators, Royal Enfield first closed its old-established Redditch plant (to be parcelled out as a trading estate, the site value of the factory being worth far more than the new owners had given for the company) then went under-ground, to produce its final model, the 736 cc Series II Interceptor, in former quarry workings in wildest Wiltshire.

The second-oldest firm in the industry (the oldest, Excelsior, had already ceased motor cycle manufacture in 1963 to produce, under Britax management, car seat belts and other accessories), Ariel closed the venerable Selly Oak works, moved in with BSA, then disappeared—save for an impossibly comic three-wheeled moped, to which BSA, the real perpetrators, had been too ashamed to apply their own trade mark. And although the crash of the BSA-Triumph group did not take place until a couple of years after the period covered by this book, the seeds of disaster had long been sown.

Now, it is all too easy to sit back and say that the Japanese swept into Britain with new and up-to-date designs, elbowed aside the obsolete British models, and helped themselves to the market. Except that it simply did not happen like that. In fact the British motor cycle market was already dead before the Japanese arrived, with many a long-established motor cycle dealer going out of business, or switching over to selling cars, the

Robin Good, on the Ariel Arrow he shared with Peter Inchley, gives Brian Setchell (650 Norton) a run for his money in the 1962 Silverstone 1000. After leading the 250 cc class for much of the distance, the Arrow finished second following a bout of electrical trouble

The ES400 was the only small-capacity Norton twin to feature electric starting

casualties even including Stan Hailwood's powerful Kings of Oxford chain.

If we must hunt for the true villain of the piece, let's call it the Affluent Society of those 'never had it so good' early 1960s. For many years following the Second World War the motor cycle was still regarded principally as working-class transport, a cheaper to run alternative to the unaffordable car. There were a few more exotic models of the type we would today term status symbols (the big Vincent vee-twins, for example, and the Ariel Square Four), but by and large the British industry earned its bread and butter with such utility jobs as the BSA C15, Triumph Tiger Cub, Royal Enfield Crusader, and James and Francis-Barnett two-strokes.

But as industry in general entered a boom period, the working man found himself with more money in his pocket, and suddenly the Austin Mini or Ford Popular were not so unaffordable, after all. This was roughly the same situation that had faced the German motor cycle industry a few years previously, when Horex, Adler, TWN and many another factory either closed, or changed to some other field (typewriters and office equipment, in the case of Adler and TWN).

In Britain, too, there were other factors affecting motor cycle sales, and not the least of these was the down-market image of the Leather Boys who haunted the caffs on city outskirts and, between playing rock n'roll on the gaudy juke-box, went off down the local by-pass for a ton-up tear-up. So maybe they

weren't true, US-style Hell's Angels. So maybe, in their own eyes, they were doing no harm to anyone. But what the ton-up crowd with their dropped-handlebar Road Rockets and T-One-Tens did to motor cycling as a whole was nobody's business.

Of course, there were always 'knockers' in certain newspapers and in TV who blew up everything larger-than-life and made a 'Shock! Horror!' spectacular of it all. Spurred on by such stories, the government of the day brought in the Hughes-Hallett Bill, effective from July, 1961, which restricted the holder of a motor cycle provisional driving licence to a machine of no more than 250 cc.

It has to be said that inexperienced youngsters, weaving in and out of the traffic on the Watford By-pass on clapped-out BSA A10s adorned with chequered go-faster tape, had brought it on themselves. But let it not be forgotten that the Hughes-Hallett Bill intended also that the age at which a lad could ride a moped should be lowered to 15 years; *that* bit has never been put into effect.

One more factor has to be considered, for successive Chancellors of the Exchequer treated the application of hire purchase restrictions, and of purchase tax itself, in yo-yo fashion, so the dealers never knew where they stood. In addition, Britain withdrew the General Agreement on Trade and Tariffs (GATT), which left the home market vulnerable to foreign markets.

If 1960 had been the high tide of motor cycle new-machine registrations, that tide was to go into the ebb with dramatic suddenness, as the monthly figures through 1961 indicated drops of up to 35 per cent below the equivalent period of 1960. It was the old Excelsior company which, early in 1962, found a loophole in the purchase tax regulations and began offering first a 150 cc roadster, and then a 98 cc lightweight, in part-assembled, finish-it-yourself kit form. The 150 cc Excelsior Universal, powered by Excelsior's own two-stroke engine, was priced at £103 19s, so saving the customer a whacking £40-worth of purchase tax.

But the firms who really latched on to the kit-form, no-purchase-tax idea were those supplying trials and scrambles machinery, headed by Sprite, a bouncy little Black Country factory headed by cheery Frank Hipkin. In turn, the importers of Bultaco and Montesa competitions machinery from Spain took up the scheme, and soon no trials or scrambles rider bothered to buy a complete, ready-built-up bike.

The close of 1961 found Associated Motor Cycles foundering in deep water, for their £219,000 profit of the previous year had turned into a thumping great £350,000 loss. Unhappily, it was true that AMC, in particular, had always been slow in perceiving market trends and responding to them. The scooter was a case in point, and Vespa and Lambretta had been allowed to gain too big a bridgehead in Britain before the home-base factories made any kind of challenge.

The attitude of AMC's top brass was that scooters would never catch on, being just a flash in the pan. Yet even AMC were at last forced into building a scooter (the 150 cc James); it embodied one or two good ideas, such as using the main frame tubes as crash bars, but it was too clumsy . . . and too late.

The two last criticisms could be levelled also at Velocette's majestic flat-twin two-stroke 250 cc Velocette Viceroy scooter, which featured car-type electric starting. Technically excellent though the specification may have been, its sheer size was enough to deter those attuned to the dainty Italian models. On the other hand, the true-born motor cyclist would not have looked at a scooter, no matter how honoured a name it bore. So at whom was the Viceroy aimed?

To the end, Velocettes were a company run by the Goodman family. Tooling up for Viceroy production had cost them far more than subsequent sales warranted, and the failure of this model was the direct cause of the collapse of the firm.

The wounds of the BSA-Triumph group were, to some degree, self-inflicted. Part of the trouble was that a number of key executives who had been with the combine for many years all reached retirement age at more or less the same time. They included home sales manager George Savage, development chief Bert Perrigo, group chairman Jack Sangster, and even Edward Turner, that very shrewd character who was a brilliant designer and an administrator of remarkable ability.

Turner's retirement took effect in 1962, but acting in a freelance capacity he was to produce one last design—a 350 cc double-overhead camshaft twin of which the prototype, ridden at

One of the less glamorous members of the 248 cc Royal Enfield family, the Wallaby was intended for sheep-herding on outback ranches in Australia

MIRA by Percy Tait, clocked 112 mph. As Turner designed it, the machine featured a train of gears to the overhead camshafts, but the model was subsequently re-engineered to incorporate an awkward right-angle chain driven camshaft. Launched with a panoply of trumpets in the dying days of BSA-Triumph it was, of course, the BSA Fury—or, if you prefer, Triumph Bandit—and it never did get into production.

Under the guidance of Harry Sturgeon, BSA-Triumph continued to flourish in the mid-1960s. The home market had all but disappeared, but overseas sales, especially to the USA, were such that the company collected the Queen's Award to Industry for their export performance, for two years in succession. Sadly, Harry Sturgeon died in 1967 after all too short a reign, and in his place the board appointed one Lionel Jofeh, late of the Sperry Gyroscope Company. From then on, the skids were under Small Heath, helped by the establishment of a wildly expensive research department based at a country mansion known as Umberslade Hall.

If we can now look across to the other side of the world, Japan ended the war with a huge home market crying out for personal powered transport. Well over forty factories came into being to plug the gap, one of them started by Mr. Soichiro Honda, who had bought a job lot of ex-Japanese Army small-capacity engines, and was soon engaged in fitting these into bicycle frames.

Competition was fierce, and by 1960 Japan was down to about ten major manufacturers, each with enormous production capacity. As their own home market became saturated, so the Japanese makers began an export drive, at first into nearby Far East markets, and later into the USA. For a while, this acted in the British industry's favour. Japanese motor cycles were small-capacity machines, and when the American purchaser of one such returned to the dealer, bitten by the bug and demanding something more powerful, the same dealer sold him a Triumph, or a BSA.

Headed by the appearance of Honda, Suzuki, Yamaha and Tohatsu models in European road racing, the Japanese machines began to infiltrate Europe and, eventually, Britain. Their marketing, however, was very different to that which had been employed by the now largely defunct British industry—mainly restricted to the weekly motor cycle press. Instead, Honda, the market leaders, took large spaces in the national newspapers, on poster hoardings, and even—an unheard-of-thing—on commercial television channels. The message was always the same: 'You Meet the Nicest People on a Honda!'

And indeed you did, because the appeal was to a new type of rider, who would never have crossed the threshold of the typical back-street motor cycle dealer's premises in a month of Sundays. But he would have no hesitation in walking into the bright High Street outlet of the Japanese franchise holder.

It may be asked why the British industry did not forsee the trend, and start building elegant little electric-start 125 cc twins, and automatic-transmission step-through scooterettes, since that was what the new public wanted. The answer is that nobody in this country ever had got fat on motor cycle manufacture, even in the boom years, and the banks were certainly not going to risk capital on the re-equipment of our factories to meet the new threat.

The British motor cycle world was ever a Cinderella industry, hammered by successive governments and clobbered by economic conditions. It was destined never to get to the Great Ball, but along the way it made some really great bikes. You'll meet many of them in this book.

Ambassador Three Star Special

The pre-war motor racing scene would appear to have been peopled by characters who were slightly larger-than-life, among whom could certainly be classed Kaye Don. In his younger days Kaye had been a regular member of the Brooklands motor cycling brigade, but by the mid-1920s he had switched to four wheels.

His particular field was record-breaking, and with a little car named the Avon-JAP, using alternative engines of 495, 731 and 986 cc, he established a variety of records; those in the 500 cc class were unbroken when Brooklands closed for good and, therefore, stand in Kaye Don's name in perpetuity.

He had his eyes on higher things, too, nothing less than the World Land Speed Record, for which reason he persuaded the Sunbeam Motor Car Company (who had constructed Major Henry Segrave's record-holder, Golden Arrow) to build him a suitable challenger, named Silver Bullet.

Regrettably, the Silver Bullet did not have quite enough energy to allow it to reach the set target, although Kaye Don did gain some consolation by taking the World Water Speed Record with his boat, *Miss England*. To finance such ambitions, Kaye had established the firm of US Concessionaires, based at Ascot, to import and service American-built Pontiac cars.

That line of business folded abruptly on the outbreak of the Second World War, but Pontiac Works were kept fully occupied with the overhaul and repair of all kinds of road transport, under governmental direction.

The return of peace saw little hope of a resumption of the import of vast and expensive American cars. Quite the opposite, indeed, for Britain now found itself desperate for foreign currency. This was 'Export or Die' time, with the limited stocks of steel and other metals being allocated only to those with a flourishing export trade.

Kaye Don felt that he could find a market for a simple and uncomplicated British lightweight motor cycle in the more far-flung areas of the world and so, in mid-1946, he registered the appropriate trade-mark of Ambassador. Not everybody in the existing British industry was happy to see a newcomer muscling-in on the scene. For example, the old-established Zenith, Cotton, and AJW factories were struggling to get back into production, using a new 500 cc side-valve vee-twin engine from J. A. Prestwich. Supplies were slow in coming through, and on a visit to the JAP works, Mr. J. O. Ball, of AJW, was not at all pleased to see one of these units being fitted to a bike bearing the hitherto-unknown name of Ambassador on the tank.

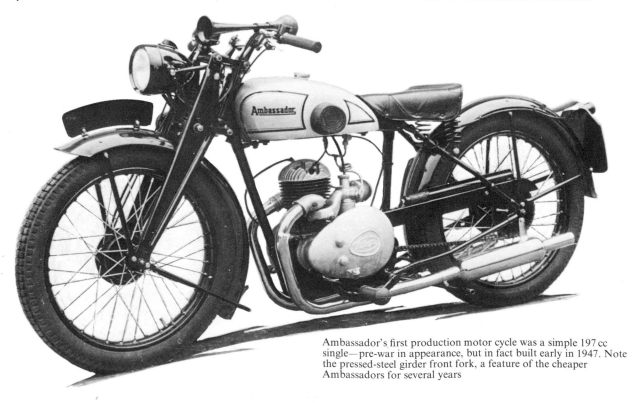

Ambassador's first production motor cycle was a simple 197 cc single—pre-war in appearance, but in fact built early in 1947. Note the pressed-steel girder front fork, a feature of the cheaper Ambassadors for several years

Nevertheless, it was not with a JAP but with a 197 cc Villiers power unit that Ambassador went into production in December, 1946. Answering the 'Export or Die' call, the makers had earmarked the entire first batch for overseas customers, the first consignment going to Argentina and the second to Ceylon.

Simple, agreed, but nobody could call that first 197 cc Ambassador pretty. It had a distinctly 'pre-war' appearance, even to the use of a pressed-steel Webb girder front fork, and rigid brazed-lug frame, and was so low-built that it looked to have negative ground clearance.

Villiers had first announced the 197 cc unit-construction engine-gear assembly—at that time called the Double Century, because it was roughly 200 cc—back in 1938, as a follow-up to their first venture into unit-construction with the 125 cc Mk. 9D. It was fitted with hand gear-change, and only James had taken it up, but few were made before the coming of war.

The new version which made its debut with the Ambassador was the Mk. 5E, still with twin exhaust pipes but now featuring foot gear-change. It was to prove one of the most successful Villiers designs of all time, not only progressing through various developments to the well-remembered Mk. 9E unit which powered a number of trials and scrambles models of the late-1950s/early-1960s period, but also forming a basis for the later 250 cc singles.

Alec Frick was the Ambassador designer, and within a year or so he had devised a rather better, welded tubular frame and, moreover, he arranged for the frames to be built in Birmingham by the Reynolds Tube Company. Previously, Reynolds' had supplied tubing only, leaving it to the motor cycle factories to make their own frames. However, during the war they had undertaken the manufacture of tubular mounting assemblies for the aircraft industry, and it was this experience that was now put to good use in the motor cycle field. What is more, Alec Frick now left Ambassador, and joined the Reynolds Tube works as a motor cycle frame designer, devising and building frames for the majority of the smaller British factories.

The Ambassador range expanded to accommodate a 147 cc Popular model and, at the other end of the scale, a 249 cc Villiers 2T twin. It was probably the last British factory to retain (on the bargain-basement Popular) a girder fork and rigid frame, albeit enterprising enough in other directions, exhibiting at Earls Court what was claimed to be (and probably was) the first British machine with electric starting—employing a starter motor mounted under the tank, and vee-belt drive to a groove around the periphery of the Villiers flywheel magneto.

Meanwhile, Ambassador noted the scooter trend, and made arrangements to import and distribute the German-made Zündapp Bella scooter and the Zündapp Combinette moped and, ostensibly, went into moped manufacture on their own account by producing, for the 1962 season, an Ambassador model with somewhat overdressed bodywork and a 50 cc Villiers 3K engine (it was, of course, just a Zündapp imported without power unit, and fitted with the Villiers at Pontiac Works).

Design by this time was under the charge of former Norton technician, Edgar Franks, and by 1960 a very attractive house-style had been achieved, as is seen on the Three Star Special of the following pages. The then-current fashion was for semi-enclosure of the rear wheel, but Ambassador did not go the whole hog (as did Francis-Barnett, with the full-skirted Cruiser 84) and, instead, evolved a kind of mini-skirt rear pressing which, in conjunction with the deeply valanced front guard, is still pleasantly eye-catching, even now.

Following pages: Fred Hibbert's 1960 Super S has the 249 cc Villiers 2T engine, but is otherwise similar to the 197 cc Three-Star single

Close-up of the 197 cc Villiers Mk. 4E engine-gear unit of the 1947 Ambassador, a revamp of the 1938 Mk. 3E unit, retaining twin exhausts but now with foot instead of hand gear change

The Ambassador story was not entirely one of unqualified success, and their reason for introducing (in October, 1960) their own 172 cc Villiers-powered scooter is a little obscure. Styling, not unnaturally, was based on the Zündapp Bella, which the firm was still importing. It was about £20 cheaper than the Bella, but that is as much as can be said for it.

Unlike most other British small manufacturers, Ambassador shunned the sporting side, and did not add a trials or scrambles model to the programme. In fact, as time went by the firm's enthusiasm for motor cycles went into a decline as, more and more, the import from France of giant Latil earth-moving equipment for open-cast mining took precedence.

The sale of the Ambassador name, jigs, and manufacturing rights to DMW, of Dudley, in 1962 was not really a surprise. The 197 cc Three Star Special was to remain available for two more seasons, still with its pressed-steel tail but now featuring a DMW-style square-tube frame loop. It was more or less badge-engineering, because towards the end the two ranges were identical, except that if you ordered a DMW it came with the familiar humpty-style tank and DMW badges, whereas the Ambassador fancier got the same bike but equipped with the more rounded tank and diamond-shape badges of the former Ascot-based marque.

During a 1930 visit to the Isle of Man TT races, Kaye Don—later the founder of the Ambassador factory—rounds Signpost Corner on a Norton

ROAD TESTS of new models

197 c.c. Ambassador

VERY ATTRACTIVELY STYLED TWO-STROKE CAPABLE OF TIRELESS PULLING: GOOD SUSPENSION, STEERING AND HANDLING: FULL MUDGUARDING

★

★

★

WITH the increased flow of two-fifties on the British market in recent times, a new rôle has fallen on the one-nine-seven. Hitherto the most powerful of the "true lightweights," it now caters for riders prepared to settle for slightly less power than they

might have in order to take advantage of a lower initial price. Viewed in that light —as a sort of keen buyer's two-fifty—the latest Ambassador Three Star Special earns full marks.

The outstanding impression after several hundred miles' riding was of the 197 c.c. Villiers Mark 9E engine-gear unit's untiring capacity for hard work. One- or two-up, buzzing along main roads or pulling hard on steep country upgrades, the Ambassador seemed capable of going on indefinitely. A Villiers silencer is fitted which means that the exhaust is commendably quiet; this tended to emphasize induction roar, particularly at wide throttle openings. Mechanical noise was confined to mild piston slap at low engine speeds.

Power delivery was smooth but marred by flutter from the rear chain at around 45 m.p.h. in top gear and at corresponding speeds in the intermediate gears. The engine has a wide torque spread and pulled well throughout the range. Two-stroking was good, even at ultra-high engine revolutions in the intermediate gears—an indication of good breathing. Threading city traffic at walking pace could be accomplished with the clutch fully home, while the model would pobble along in top gear on a fractionally open throttle without transmission snatch.

On one occasion the test model was ridden hard on a 120-mile non-stop trip, during which long main-road hills were taken on full throttle in top or third gear as necessary. There was no sign of distress. The power unit remained oil-tight throughout. Calibrated to 70 m.p.h. the Smiths speedometer (which has no trip recorder) read 2 m.p.h. fast at 30 m.p.h. and 3 m.p.h. fast at 50 m.p.h.

Closing the carburettor strangler ensured first-kick starting from cold, after which the strangler could be opened immediately. Starting when the engine was warm required no particular technique.

Fuel consumption, overall, worked out at about 80 m.p.g. Tank capacity, at 3½ gallons, therefore permitted 250-mile runs to be completed without a refuelling stop. The filler cap is commendably large and, positioned centrally, allows the fuel level on both sides of the tank arch to be readily seen. The cap is effectively sealed, so that the top of the tank remained

Above: The handlebar is concealed by a metal pressing. The tank filler cap is sensibly large, enabling the level to be easily checked. Right: Underseat view showing the battery and tool roll neatly stowed. Note the ingenious rubber mounting for the rear of the tank

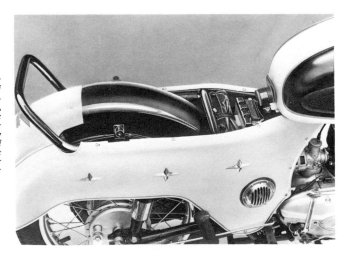

Three Star Special

pleasantly free from oil stains. The pull-on fuel tap, which incorporates a reserve position, was difficult to operate with a gloved hand.

Robust and with wide-spaced feet, the centre stand was easy to operate and supported the model safely, even on steepish cambers. Rear-chain adjustment was required only once during 900 miles. Though not "oil bath," the enclosure is markedly effective.

The riding position would be improved if the footrests were about three inches farther to the rear, to allow the rider's feet to take a greater proportion of his weight than is possible with the present location. Adjustment is provided, but results in the footrests being lower, thus allowing them to ground on corners. The handlebar shape gives a satisfactory wrist angle, and the generously dimensioned dual-seat is comfortable whether it is used one- or two-up. Removal of the seat (by withdrawing two screws with a coin) exposes the top of the battery and the recess containing the tools.

Rear springing is by a pivoted fork controlled by Girling spring-and-hydraulic units with three-position adjustment. The front fork is undamped. Characteristics of both the front and rear systems were such that there was no pitching even on undulating surfaces. Changes of lock could be made swiftly and with remarkably little conscious effort.

Braking was progressive, and adequate, although the front brake was a shade spongy. The rear-brake pedal is so positioned that its pad lies directly beneath the rider's left foot. Front-brake and clutch levers, the pivot blocks for both of which are welded to the handlebar, needed a long reach.

The gear-change pedal could be moved by merely pivoting the right foot on its footrest. Gear changing was positive and noiseless—at all times simplicity itself.

Pedal movement was short and light. Neutral could be selected without fumbling from bottom or second gear when the machine was stationary and the engine idling. The ratios proved excellently matched to the power characteristics and the closeness of third and top (7.74 and 6.2 to 1) enabled third to be used

Left: Access to the contact breaker is easily gained by removal of three screws and a cover. Right: A detail shot of the rear-brake cross-over shaft and braker-light mechanism

immediately traffic, gradient or headwind brought a drop in speed.

An indicated 45 m.p.h. suited the model best when journeys of any length were undertaken. Main-road hills normally needed no gear lower than third. On steep upgrades encountered on minor roads it was rarely necessary to use bottom gear except for restarting or when haulked two-up.

Restarting on a 1 in 6 hill was accomplished in bottom gear with very little fuss. Indeed, the clutch could be fully engaged as soon as the machine was under way. Heavier in operation than was strictly necessary, the clutch freed at all times,

even after a number of standing-start tests. It took up the drive progressively and required no adjustment.

After-dark riding was very pleasant. The driving beam ensured that daylight cruising speeds could be maintained, and that held good whether the direct or battery lighting was in use. With the handlebar-mounted dip switch in the dipped position, the cut-off was well-defined and dazzle-free. Mounted simply in two ears on the top fork covers, the headlamp is easily adjustable. Twin electric horns are located in the rear panelling (one on each side facing forward); they were adequately powerful

The ammeter is located on the left upper face of the headlamp shell; it indicated that the flywheel generator balanced the maximum load (all lights on) at 30 m.p.h.

Protection from road filth was first-class. The valancing of the front mudguard extends almost to the bottom of each fork leg. That feature, and the rear enclosure, did much to trap water thrown up by the tyres. More than that, the valancing and mid-section enclosure, combined with the smart black-and-white finish, a "three-dimensional" tank motif and the discreet use of chromium plating, all contribute towards making the Ambassador a most eyeable model.

▲▲▲▲▲▲▲▲▲▲▲▲▲▲▲▲▲▲▲▲▲▲ *Specification* ▲▲▲▲▲▲▲▲▲▲▲▲▲▲▲▲▲▲▲▲▲▲

ENGINE: Villiers 197 c.c. (59 x 72 mm) Mark 9E single-cylinder two-stroke. Roller big-end bearing; crankshaft supported in a roller bearing on the right-hand side and two ball bearings on the left. Light-alloy cylinder head; cast-iron barrel. Compression ratio, 7.25 to 1. Petroil lubrication; mixture 20 to 1.

CARBURETTOR: Villiers S.25 with wire-gauze air filter incorporating a strangler.

TRANSMISSION: Villiers four-speed, foot-controlled gear box in unit with the engine. Gear ratios: bottom, 17.95 to 1; second, 10.85 to 1; third, 7.74 to 1; top, 6.2 to 1. Multi-plate clutch with bonded, moulded linings running in oil. Primary chain, ⅜ x 0.225in oil-bath case; rear chain ½ x 0.305in enclosed in pressed-steel case. Engine r.p.m. at 30 m.p.h. in top gear, 2,650.

IGNITION AND LIGHTING: Villiers flywheel magneto with lighting coils. Exide 6-volt 7.5 ampere-hour battery charged through rectifier; 5½-diameter Miller headlamp with prefocus light unit; 30/24 watt main bulb.

PETROIL CAPACITY: 3½ gallons.

TYRES: Dunlop 3.25 x 17in studded front and rear.

BRAKES: 6in diameter front and rear.

SUSPENSION: Ambassador undamped telescopic front fork with two-rate springing. Pivoted rear fork controlled by Girling adjustable spring-and-hydraulic telescopic units.

WHEELBASE: 51in unladen. Ground clearance 6½in unladen.

SEAT: Ambassador dual-seat; unladen height 31in.

WEIGHT: 272 lb fully equipped and with one gallon of petroil.

PRICE: £137 10s; with purchase tax (in Great Britain only) £165 15s 2d.

ROAD TAX: £1 17s 6d a year.

MANUFACTURERS: Ambassador Motor Cycles. Ltd., Pontiac Works. Ascot, Berks.

PERFORMANCE DATA

MEAN MAXIMUM SPEED: Bottom: 26 m.p.h.
Second: 39 m.p.h.
Third: 49 m.p.h.
Top: 55 m.p.h.

HIGHEST ONE-WAY SPEED: 60 m.p.h. (conditions: strong following wind; rider wearing two-piece suit and overboots).

MEAN ACCELERATION:

	10-30 m.p.h.	20-40 m.p.h.	30-50 m.p.h.
Second	10.2 sec	—	—
Third	—	14 sec	—
Top	—	16 sec	18.2 sec

Mean speed at end of quarter mile from rest: 53 m.p.h.
Mean time to cover standing quarter mile: 23.2 sec.

PETROIL CONSUMPTION: At 30 m.p.h., 96 m.p.g. At 40 m.p.h., 82 m.p.g.

BRAKING: From 30 m.p.h. to rest, 38ft (surface dry tarmac).

TURNING CIRCLE: 12ft 6in.

MINIMUM NON-SNATCH SPEED: 18 m.p.h. in top gear.

WEIGHT PER C.C.: 1.32 lb.

Matchless G12 de Luxe

They always were a contrary lot, down at the AMC factory in Plumstead Road, Woolwich. For years they scorned the services of the specialist suspension firms and when, at long last, they did adopt proper Girling rear damper units, AMC insisted that these should be made with special yoke ends to fit their frames, rather than modify their frames to accommodate standard dampers.

Except on their two-stroke engines used by James and Francis-Barnett (and even then, AMC gave up eventually and shipped the parts up to Wolverhampton, so that Villiers could put them together properly), they never did go in for full unit-construction of engine and gearbox.

When it came to following the lead set by Triumph, and adding a vertical twin to the range, they had to be different by giving theirs a centre bearing, so that the engine 'could operate to very high rpm while remaining rigid'. Don't you believe it! Former Midland editor of *Motor Cycling*, Bernal Osborne had one of the first Matchless twins—indeed, *the* first one ever to be sold on the home market—as his staff machine, and the vibration was far worse than that of any Triumph, Ariel, BSA or Norton twin.

The crankshaft was a massive one-piece casting in nodular iron, supported at each side in roller main bearings, but the centre bearing (which served to locate the shaft) was a Vandervell thin-wall shell through which was fed oil under pressure, to be delivered through drillways to the big-end bearings.

The designer was Phil Walker, and the first of the range was the 498 cc Model G9 Super Clubman introduced as a 1948 Earls Court Show surprise. Unfortunately, AMC were under the delusion that their bottom-end assembly, designed for touring work, would serve equally well for racing purposes, but they were given a rude awakening when the engine of the first G45 racer (essentially a beefed-up G9 unit, installed in the rolling chassis of an AJS Model 7R Boy Racer) was undergoing final bench-testing, prior to being despatched to the Isle of Man so that Robin Sherry could ride it in the 1951 Senior Manx Grand Prix. When the motor was given full throttle, the cast-iron crankshaft snapped just behind the driving sprocket, and the broken shaft, complete with test-bed coupling, went whizzing

Paddy Driver (646 cc Matchless) leading Phil Read on a battered-looking 650 cc Norton damaged in a spill, at the 1963 Oulton Park 1000 km race

round the test shop carving chunks out of the concrete walls. A steel crankshaft was hurriedly substituted, and Robin Sherry finished a creditable fourth in the race, but admitted to being shaken to a jelly by the vibration.

However, the shimmy-shakes were brought under control in later seasons, and for 1956 a bigger roadster twin, the 592 cc G11, joined the programme. The reason, said the makers was 'a demand for increased power from overseas markets, particularly the USA, and from sidecar drivers at home who require greater torque than is available from 500 cc'. The stroke of both models was retained at 72·88 mm, but the bore of the bigger engine was 72 mm, as against the 66 mm of the G9.

As explained earlier, AMC's own rear damper units were exchanged for Girling units (with special yoke ends) in 1957, and the next season brought a new cast-light-alloy primary chaincase.

In April, 1958, *Motor Cycle's* technical editor, Vic Willoughby, had a lot of fun hurtling around the Motor Industry Research Association's banked-bends test track near Nuneaton on a fully-equipped 592 cc Matchless G11 Sports Twin—headlamp, registration plates, even a licence holder—to cover 102·926 mph in an hour from a standing start.

Even so, the Americans wanted yet more power, and that set the AMC factory a poser. Because the cylinder centre lines are a set distance apart, there is a limit on how far one can bore-out a cylinder, and that limit had been reached with the G11. The only alternative was to retain the 72 mm bore of the G11, but fit a crankshaft with a longer (79·3 mm) stroke.

So, at last, in 1959 the 646 cc G12 family was evolved—four models, comprising G12 Standard (with alternator electrics), G12 de Luxe, G12CS, and G12CSR, the last two featuring higher compression ratio, siamese pipes, and titivated porting. The major change for 1960 was a new duplex frame.

Around this time, marketing of AJS and Matchless models in the USA was left to the tender mercies of the Joe Berliner

South African racing star of the 1960s, Paddy Driver pilots a G12 Matchless twin prepared by Tom Kirby in the 1964 Thruxton 500-miler

Corporation, at whose door can be laid the blame for the horrific juke-box tank badges which erupted in 1962. Nor was that all, because the catalogue became spattered with model names—which, naturally, the faithful public flatly refused to use. The de Luxe and G12CS variants were dropped and, instead, there were just the G12 Majestic, and G12CSR Monarch—the latter better known to the lads of the village as the Sportstwin or, from its catalogue designation letters, the 'Coffee Shop Racer'.

For 1963, the wheel diameter was reduced to 18 in and there was a choice of 10·25 to 1 pistons, 'suitable for marathon racing'. That was significant, because by then the G12CSR was featuring in long-distance production machine racing. Quite notably, too, with Paddy Driver and Joe Dunphy as the winning co-riders in the Bemsee 1000-kilometre event of May, 1963. They might well have made it a double by winning the Thruxton 500-Miles, had not a broken chain put them out of the reckoning. (Success had come at Thruxton in 1960, when Ron Langston and Don Chapman romped home with a 646 cc AJS twin—which was just a Matchless with a different timing cover motif.)

In the 1964 Thruxton 500-Miles, Paddy Driver was again the hero, this time sharing the saddle of Tom Kirby's G12CSR with Roger Hunter. For hour after hour the Matchless was involved in a thorough ding-dong with Triumph testers Percy Tait and Fred Swift, on a Bonneville. But at just after 4 pm, with 159 laps completed and having led for four hours, the Matchless was pushed into the pits. Paddy Driver thought that the primary chain had broken; an ominous hole in the crankcase told a different tale.

Because of dire financial troubles, the writing was now on the wall for Matchless, and 1966 was the final year of production of the vertical twin. With the collapse of the AMC empire, Norton Villiers stepped in to pick up some of the pieces, and for a short time the Plumstead works came back to a semblance of life under the new subsidiary name of Norton-Matchless Ltd. But the twin had gone, and the Matchless name survived on just one model, a single-cylinder scrambler. Then that, too, vanished.

Alone among British vertical-twin four-strokes, the Matchless employed a centre crankshaft bearing, housed in a divider plate sandwiched between the two crankcase halves. Cylinder barrels, and cylinder heads, were independent castings

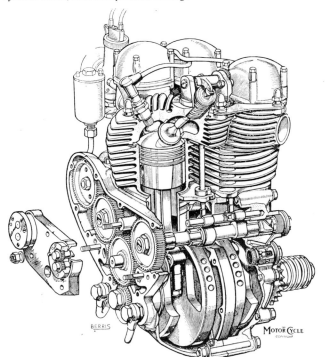

646 c.c. Matchless G12 de Luxe

Fast but Tractable Super-touring Parallel Twin with a Liking for the Open Road

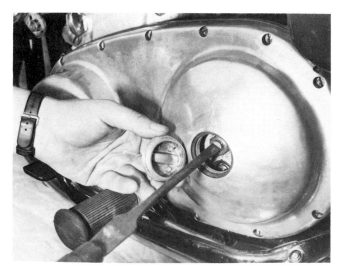

Ready access to the clutch thrust rod adjusting screw and locknut is obtainable after removing a screwed cap in the primary chaincase

DOCILITY and high performance make a rare combination. Top-gear tractability you can have, speed you can have; but both? Yes, both! In the latest 646 c.c. Matchless G12 de Luxe you can. A bulldog with all the get-up-and-go of a greyhound, this is a twin to which everything comes alike, whether it be a gentle potter around the lanes at 30 m.p.h. or a blast along M1 at 80 m.p.h. on half throttle.

From a near-walking pace in bottom gear, juicy, beefy power is on tap right through the range—and that is a characteristic which diehards say vanished with the big vee-twins of old. Above all, the charm of the Matchless lies in the way such urge is developed. There is commendably little fuss, and speed builds up smoothly and with deceptive rapidity.

With such ample power in hand high point-to-point averages could readily, and safely, be maintained; a mere whiff more of gas and the model would sail past slower-moving traffic, so that full advantage could be taken of gaps in the vehicle stream.

Response to the throttle was instantaneous. From 25 m.p.h. in second, a tweak of the grip was sufficient to send the speedometer needle scurrying round to the 50 mark; then up to third gear, and 70 would arrive in a satisfyingly short time before top was engaged. On the other hand, if there was no urgency about the ride, top could be held to well down below 30 m.p.h.—and the engine would pull away smoothly, unobtrusively, with not a hint of transmission roughness.

Long main-road gradients meant not a thing. Steeper hills were a joy to tackle. Second gear sufficed for the really severe stuff, while a standing start on the 1 in 3 test hill at the M.I.R.A. proving ground was easily accomplished in bottom.

Though the engine was exceptionally smooth at speeds up to 60 m.p.h. (or 63 m.p.h. if the speedometer reading was accepted) beyond that some vibration could be felt through the handlebar and footrests—though it was not serious enough to deter one from holding the eighties for mile after mile; for some unaccountable reason the tremor seemed to disappear when accelerating hard. By allowing the model sufficient time to gather speed, a genuine 100 m.p.h. was reached on M1 on several occasions with the rider adopting a slight crouch to reduce windage.

The engine seemed perfectly willing to take harsh treatment indefinitely, with the only external evidence of hard driving a slight seepage from the oil-tank filler cap. If the tank was topped up much

Drive-side aspect of the well-proportioned, six-fifty twin power unit

Layout of the handlebar looks particularly clean. Lighting and ignition switches are in the headlamp shell

above the minimum level, excess oil blown out through the crankcase breather left a film on the rear of the machine. (However, in 750 miles, only a pint of oil was required to restore the level in the tank.)

From the twin megaphone-type silencers came a deep-throated growl which, though pleasing to an enthusiast's ears, was perhaps a shade too loud for these days.

As to be expected with a coil-ignition model, starting was "first time, every time" provided that, when cold, the carburettor was flooded lightly and the air lever closed; within a few seconds the lever could be fully opened, when the engine would settle down to a slow and reliable tickover. One minor crib concerned the very light action of the ignition switch of the test model. Mounted

on the right of the headlamp shell, it was possible to brush against the switch, unknowingly turn it on and so cause the battery to run flat.

So that the full performance of the G12 may be enjoyed, some care should be taken in tailoring the riding position to suit, and for that reason the very wide range of adjustment of the footrests, rear-brake pedal and gear lever was appreciated.

The controls are well laid out and convenient to operate. Horn push and dip switch are within easy reach of the left thumb (though a more far-reaching horn blast would be an advantage on such a roadburner as this). Handlebar grips are of plastic, and it was felt that a bolder patterning might have been more comfortable, in addition to affording greater friction.

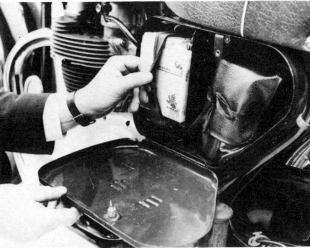

A roomy box on the left of the model, with hinged lid and coin-slot Dzus fastener, contains the battery and tool roll

Following pages: the 650 cc G12 Matchless twin was a development of the 600 cc design, of which this is a 1958 G11CS example (*National Motorcycle Museum*)

The dual-seat is generously dimensioned and after a non-stop two-up trip of over 200 miles, neither the rider nor female passenger felt any trace of stiffness or fatigue—and when the passenger volunteers a remark that her half of the seat is comfortable, that can be counted as high praise indeed!

A man-size mount, the Matchless tips the scales at 420 lb and so is a little too bulky to be thrown around as though it were a two-fifty. Nevertheless, once a line through a corner was chosen, it would adhere to that line without deviation and was particularly stable if the power was fed in through the corner. Low-speed balance was good, and it was easy to weave the model through slow-moving traffic.

Straight-ahead steering was impressively positive, though at speeds below 35 m.p.h. a trace of front-wheel flutter could be felt on very smooth surfaces. Cornering on unusually bumpy surfaces produced slight (although never troublesome) yawing, but in general the suspension was well up to the job of ironing-out road shocks without pitching.

Like the engine, the clutch did not object to abuse, and engaged the drive smoothly with a pleasantly light handlebar-lever action. When the engine was allowed to idle slowly, bottom gear engagement was noiseless. Movement of the gear lever was rather heavier than is usual with an A.M.C. gear box; this was noticeable on the upward change from second to third. The ratios matched the engine characteristics perfectly.

Smooth, powerful, and reasonably light to operate, the brakes were capable of making the tyres squeal without locking the wheels. The rear brake drum was unaffected by water, but a downpour lessened the effectiveness of the front brake; however, the full power returned after a few minutes of running with the brake lightly applied.

Rather more intensity of light from the main beam of the headlamp would have permitted higher cruising speeds to be maintained at night. The cut-off on dip was adequate and prevented oncoming drivers from being dazzled.

The only maintenance required during the test period was one adjustment of the rear chain after 600 miles. Accessibility to the power unit and cycle parts is first class and normal routine tasks could be carried out quickly and simply. The Matchless has one of the most comprehensive tool kits to be found on any machine.

That's the Matchless G12 de Luxe, a really robust twin with well-bred manners but all the punch of a prizefighter. The beef is pedigree, and handsome enough to win all the rosettes that may be going.

Handsome fast tourer from a famous stable, the Matchless G12 de Luxe has a duplex cradle frame

SPECIFICATION

ENGINE: Matchless 646 c.c. (72 x 79.3mm) overhead-valve parallel twin. Crankshaft supported in one plain and two roller bearings; plain big-end bearings. Aluminium-alloy cylinder heads. Compression ratio, 7.5 to 1. Dry sump lubrication; oil-tank capacity, four pints.

CARBURETTOR: Amal Monobloc with air slide operated by lever on handlebar.

IGNITION and LIGHTING: Coil ignition. Lucas RM15 alternator driven by crankshaft, charging 6-volt, 13 amp-hour battery through rectifier; emergency start switching. Lucas 7in-diameter pre-focus light unit with 30/24-watt main bulb and integral pilot light.

TRANSMISSION: A.M.C. four-speed gear box with positive-stop foot control. Gear ratios: bottom, 12.23 to 1; second, 8.15 to 1; third, 5.85 to 1; top, 4.79 to 1. Multi-plate clutch with bonded friction faces. Primary chain, ⅜ x 0.305in in cast-aluminium oil-bath case. Final drive by ⅝ x ⅜in chain with guard over top run. Engine r.p.m. at 30 m.p.h. in top gear, 1,825.

FUEL CAPACITY: 4¼ gallons.

TYRES: Dunlop; front, 3.25 x 19in ribbed; rear, 3.50 x 19in Universal.

BRAKES: 7½in-diameter front, 6½in rear; finger adjusters.

SUSPENSION: A.M.C. Teledraulic front fork with two-way hydraulic damping. Pivoted rear fork controlled by adjustable Girling spring units with hydraulic damping.

WHEELBASE: 55½in unladen. Ground clearance, 6in unladen.

SEAT: A.M.C. dual-seat; unladen height, 31in.

WEIGHT: 420 lb fully equipped with full oil tank and approximately one gallon of petrol.

PRICE: £221 6s 11d; with purchase tax (in Great Britain only), £267.

ROAD TAX: £4 10s a year; £1 13s for four months.

MAKERS: Matchless Motor Cycles, Plumstead Road, London, S.E.18.

PERFORMANCE DATA

(Obtained at the Motor Industry Research Association's proving ground Lindley Leicestershire.)

MEAN MAXIMUM SPEED: Bottom: *50 m.p.h.
Second: *75 m.p.h.
Third: 88 m.p.h.
Top: 95 m.p.h.
* Valve float occurring.

HIGHEST ONE-WAY SPEED: 97 m.p.h. (conditions: light three-quarter breeze; rider wearing two-piece suit and overboots).

MEAN ACCELERATION:

	10-30 m.p.h.	20-40 m.p.h.	30-50 m.p.h.
Bottom	2.6 sec	2.8 sec	3.4 sec
Second	3.8 sec	3.6 sec	3.6 sec
Third	—	5.0 sec	5.6 sec
Top	—	7.2 sec	6.6 sec

Mean speed at end of quarter-mile from rest: 82 m.p.h.
Mean time to cover standing quarter-mile: 16.4 se

PETROL CONSUMPTION: At 30 m.p.h., 64 m.p.g.; at 40 m.p.h., 62 m.p.g.; at 50 m.p.h. 59 m.p.g.; at 60 m.p.h., 51 m.p.g.

BRAKING: From 30 m.p.h. to rest, 34ft (surface, dry tarmac).

TURNING CIRCLE: 15ft 6in.

MINIMUM NON-SNATCH SPEED: 18 m.p.h. in top gear.

WEIGHT PER C.C.: 0.65 lb.

Royal Enfield Constellation

For many years the biggest-capacity vertical twin in production in Britain, Royal Enfield's mighty Constellation never quite made it to the top of the Superbike league, although that was not for lack of effort on the part of Scotland's heroic Bob McIntyre. More about that later, but first a look at the Connie's family tree.

It was a matter of evolution rather than design, and it all began with the Royal Enfield 500 Twin (by Ted Pardoe and Tony Wilson-Jones) which was first shown at the 1948 London Show. Keeping to the same conception of a nodular-iron, one-piece crankshaft, independent cylinder barrels so deeply spigoted into the crankcase that they were almost oil-cooled, and independent cylinder heads, the original 496 cc design was stretched to 692 cc for 1953, so producing the Meteor, a rather woolly animal intended primarily for sidecar haulage.

However, there was a demand, particularly from the USA, for a machine with more performance. And so the Super Meteor was introduced in 1956, while at the same time the Redditch technicians were evolving something rather better.

Although the British public first heard of the 692 cc Constellation in April, 1958, in fact it had been in production for export markets for nearly a year, and the bugs had already been shaken out. The Connie was more than a revamped Super Meteor, for it employed shell-type big-end bearings running on $1\frac{7}{8}$-in diameter crank throws (instead of running the rods directly on the pins as before). This design change had meant a bigger crankcase, but since the old crankcase dies were starting to wear out, anyway, it was as good an opportunity as any to invest in new dies. Larger valves, sportier cams, a higher compression ratio and a single Amal TT carburettor all helped to boost the power output to 51 bhp at 6,250 rpm, and to cope with all this extra power there was a hefty clutch, operated by scissors-action levers housed within the primary chaincase.

April may have seemed the wrong time to announce a new model, but the reason was that the prestigious Thruxton 500-mile race was due to be run in June, and success there would have given the Connie a flying start. Five machines were entered for the race, each being shared by a pair of riders: Bob McIntyre and Derek Powell; Brian Newman and Ken James; Alan Rutherford and Ernie Washer; Don Williams and Geoff Shekell; and Don Chapman and Jack Hill.

In the early stages of the event Royal Enfield hopes were high, with Bob Mac going straight into the lead, and taking the award for the first machine to cover 100 miles. But coming up fast was the determined pairing of Mike Hailwood and Dan Shorey, on a Triumph Tiger 110. Despite slicker pitwork by the Triumph's crew, the Constellation seemed to have the race in the bag, until

Ultimate vertical twin from Royal Enfield was the sporting 736 cc Interceptor, enlarged from the Constellation and seen here in 1964 trim with chromium-plated tank and mudguards

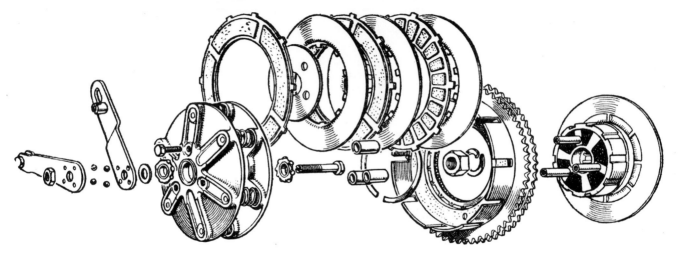

Components of the unique Constellation clutch. Operation is external through scissors-action levers, one fixed and one moving; when the outer lever is operated four interposed balls ride up the ramps of their indents and so the lever moves laterally also

the bike came into the pits for work to be done on a leaking fuel tank.

The stop was of 3 min 15 sec duration, and when Bob got back into the race he began to claw back 3 sec a lap on the Triumph. The only snag was that there was not enough race distance left, and so the Royal Enfield had to settle for runner-up spot, just half a minute astern of the winning Tiger 110. Behind McIntyre and Powell, Brian Newman and Ken James claimed third. The Williams/Shekell and Chapman/Hill teams both finished, and only the Rutherford/Washer machine dropped out.

There was no major change for 1959, except that an Airflow-fairing version was listed. Came the Thruxton 500-Miles again, with Bob McIntyre partnered now by Eric Hinton. Again the Constellation went straight into the lead, but became an early casualty when Bob dropped the model, coming through the chicane.

For the 1960 Thruxton 500-Miles, Bob took Alan Rutherford as his partner. This time it really did look like success for the Royal Enfield, and Bob and Alan were leading the field by *two laps* when trouble struck. Earlier, the nipple had pulled off the lower end of the clutch cable, but Bob pressed on, clutchless, until the end of the cable somehow tangled itself in the primary chain, locked the transmission, and pitched off poor old Bob at high speed.

There was no better luck in the 1961 event, which took place the same week as the road test which follows was published. Now Bob Mac had, as his riding mate, fellow-Scot Alastair King. Yet again the Royal Enfield took an immediate lead, with Bob in the saddle, until a connecting rod decided to come up for air—through the sump—at an estimated 110 mph. Again Bob Mac was sent skating down the track, and this time enough was enough. It was his final try for Thruxton honours.

Although all single-cylinder Royal Enfields were built at Redditch, all twin-cylinder engines had been made, almost from the start, deep underground in the factory converted from old quarry workings at Upper Westwood, near Bradford-on-Avon, Wilts. There, from 1960 onward, all Constellation crankshafts were balanced both statically and dynamically, which accounts for the smooth running of the big engine. But it was more than that because, in the interests of free-revving, lighter pistons were now in use, while a pair of Amal Monobloc carburettors looked after induction, and a new flap-valve crankcase breather was incorporated in the drive-side crankshaft end.

Changes for 1961 included a return to a conventional clutch

operating mechanism. Also, there was a rear mudguard-cum-seat base in glass fibre, wide enough to shroud the upper horizontal tubes of the seat sub-frame. Only minor changes were listed for the 1962 season, probably because the Constellation was by then on its way out.

October, 1962, brought a still bigger Royal Enfield twin, the 736 cc Interceptor, and this too had been in production for export for several months before its release to home purchasers. Ostensibly, the Constellation remained in the catalogue, but in sidecar trim only, and presumably just as a means of using up existing stocks of parts.

The last twin of all (indeed, the last British-built machine to carry the Enfield name) was Reg Thomas' completely redesigned Interceptor Series 2 of 1969. But by then, the Redditch works had already closed and production was concentrated at the Bradford-on-Avon caverns. The makers were now Enfield Precision Engineers Ltd, an offshoot (like NVT) of the Manganese Bronze empire. With Norton Commando front forks and instrumentation, Amal Concentric carburettors, 12-volt electrics, wet-sump oiling and searing performance, it was the finest Enfield of them all. But it was much, much too late.

Massively constructed, the Royal Enfield Constellation engine was not true unit-construction, the separate gearbox being bolted to the rear of the crankcase assembly. The two camshafts were driven by chain, tensioned by a jockey sprocket on an adjustable quadrant

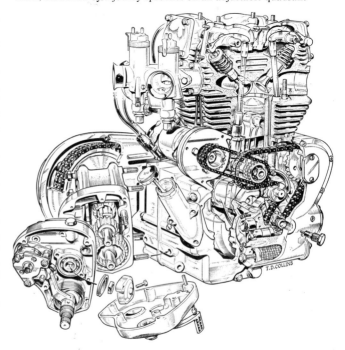

692 c.c. Royal Enfield Constellation

A Well-mannered Roadburner with Tremendous Punch and Ultra-high Cruising Speeds

FIND a connoisseur with sporting tastes and the widest possible experience and you have a rider who knows and loves the incomparable thrill of a high-geared big twin. A few years ago enthusiasts of that ilk were satisfied with nothing but the now-obsolescent 1,000 c.c. vee-twin. Its mighty punch made smaller machines seem puny while the effortlessness of its hill climbing and 90 m.p.h. cruising had to be experienced to be believed. Crisp and stirring, its exhaust note was an ever-present melody, devoid of offence for bystanders.

For those who crave that level of performance there is nothing in the present-day crop of parallel twins that approaches it more closely than the 692 c.c. twin-carburettor Royal Enfield Constellation. True, with comparable power from a smaller engine, the Royal Enfield pulls a lower top gear than the vee-twins; even so, its 4.44 to 1 ratio is higher than that of any other big parallel twin—and the Constellation is not overgeared. Indeed its low- and middle-range punch is its most endearing trait; which is high praise in a machine capable of holding 100 m.p.h. with the rider normally seated.

Tweak the grip on the Constellation and you get instantaneous, full-blooded acceleration even though the initial revs may be little above idling speed. And though the high gearing lends deception to the pick-up, the power is not vicious. Surging and abundant, yes; but smooth and easily controlled. There is as much power on tap as most ordinary riders can handle but no excuse for embarrassment; you get as much as you call for with the twistgrip.

Slick getaways require no great clutch slipping. Even on the quarter-mile standing-start acceleration tests the clutch was fully home in next to no time. And the same went for a restart on a 1 in 3 climb, so much torque has the engine at low revs.

Much of the test mileage was covered in strong winds but except for absolute maximum speed and the ultimate 5 m.p.h. of cruising speed, the practical effect on the Constellation's performance was negligible. Ridden two-up into a moderate wind, the Enfield held 85 to 90 m.p.h. indefinitely on half throttle with 96 to 98 m.p.h. on tap

Just behind the timing chest is the oil filler cap (with dip stick attached). The valve covers can be removed without disturbing the tank

Left: The dual-seat is large and well shaped; below it is a sturdy lifting handle on each side. On the right can be seen the exhaust-pipe layout. The contact breaker is very accessible and the chaincase cover retained by one nut. Extreme right: Control layout. Particularly appreciated for signalling one's approach was the large and easily reached headlamp switch

whenever the grip was fully opened.

Without a passenger, similar results were obtained against a very stiff wind; while with a following wind the length of M1 was covered at 95 to 100 m.p.h. on half throttle. Maintaining speed on long main-road climbs was simply a matter of using more throttle.

When the performance data were logged at the M.I.R.A. proving ground there was a very strong cross wind gusting to 32 m.p.h. The mean and fastest speeds of 104 and 106 m.p.h. recorded in those conditions are equivalent to still-air speeds of 109 and 111 m.p.h. respectively. Incidentally, an electronic check on the speedometer showed it to be near-enough accurate at 30 m.p.h., 1 m.p.h. fast at 40 m.p.h. and 2 m.p.h. fast from 50 to 90 m.p.h.

Peak-power engine revs of 6,250 are equivalent to 40, 60, 81 and 112 m.p.h. in the four gears, and valve-float speeds were 20 per cent higher in bottom, second and third. Normally, however, upward changes were made at speeds no higher than about 30, 50 and 70 m.p.h. because of unpleasant vibration felt through the seat. The tremor could also be felt from 95 m.p.h. upward in top gear but was not troublesome when a passenger was carried.

Though petrol consumption was on the heavy side at low speeds it dropped to an average level from 50 m.p.h. upward. When the machine was ridden really hard the all-in rate of a shade under 50 m.p.g. was about what one would expect, though oil consumption rose to approximately 1,000 m.p.g.

For a roadburner, the Constellation has an unusually low third gear—some 36 per cent below top. Both performance and the downward change into third would benefit from a reduction of the gap to about 20 to 25 per cent. When made at high speed, the change required a good blip of the throttles and firm pressure on the pedal if engagement was to be certain.

That apart, all changes were positive and clean; pedal movement was short and slightly stiff. A heel-operated neutral finder is fitted but was not normally used because no difficulty was experienced in selecting neutral with the gear pedal. Only the faintest jerk accompanied the engagement of bottom gear with the engine idling slowly. A trifle heavy to withdraw, the clutch took up the drive very sweetly, freed completely and never showed any sign of overheating.

Even when set in the lowest position consistent with not fouling the right footrest hanger on upward changes, the gear pedal was slightly too high for downward changes to be made without lifting the foot from the rest. Putting a downward set in the pedal shank cured the bother.

All the other controls were well sited except for the horn push—too far inboard on the left side of the handlebar to be reached really quickly. Since the separate dip switch is very handy to the left thumb, a combined horn button and dip switch would solve the problem. The horn note, however, was much too feeble to be effective at any but very low speeds.

By and large the riding position proved comfortable; the set of the handlebar gave the very slight forward lean required for really high speeds while a useful chock was formed by the raised rear half of the dual-seat. For all that, a more rearward footrest setting would be a boon in relaxing the grip needed on the handlebar at sustained high speeds.

At the cost of passing on some of the more severe road jolts to the rider, the very firm front and rear springing combined to make wallowing almost unknown and to keep it well in check even when the Constellation was forced round fast, bumpy bends at high speeds with a passenger and full fuel load. Bend swinging was first class and only the most exuberant banking

Below left: The front-brake control casings are anchored in a pivoted bracket on the lever. In the middle is the full-width hub housing the dual brakes. The remaining picture shows one of the snail-cam chain adjusters and the knurled sleeve for adjusting the Armstrong suspension strut

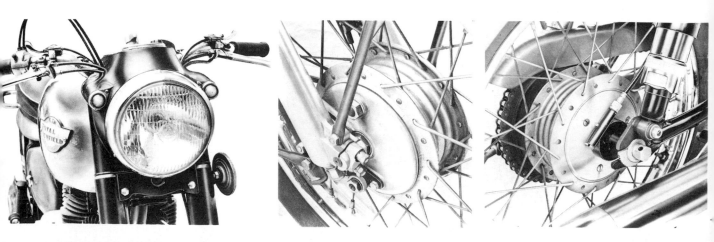

caused the footrest rubbers to graze the road.

For a machine of such speed and weight a little more bite in the brakes would be appreciated—and slightly lighter operation. When the Enfield was ridden in continuous rain or on drenched roads it was necessary to dry out the rear brake by periodic application if its efficiency was to be kept up to par.

Provided the carburettors were neither over- nor under-flooded, cold starting was generally achieved at the first kick. In extremely hot weather it was sufficient merely to close the air lever and not touch the float tickler; at other times a dab on the tickler was a good thing. Either way the ignition was best half retarded to prevent a kick-back and the twistgrip opened a shade towards the end of the pedal swing. No excessive effort was required to spin the engine over compression and the air lever could be opened wide as soon as the engine fired.

Once the engine was thoroughly warm,

full retard was needed to bring idling speed down to the tick-tock level; and precise setting of the throttle stops was essential if the cylinders were to share the running equally.

The Constellation is one of the last few super-sports machines to retain manual ignition control; and since the lever was used solely for starting and idling, auto-advance would be a welcome simplification. Pinking was never experienced on the super-premium petrols used throughout the test.

Routine maintenance was simpler than average, the contact-breaker points and valve-clearance adjusters being particularly accessible. Unusually, the valve clearances can be checked and adjusted easily without lifting the petrol tank.

It was no surprise that the duplex primary chain called for no adjustment in nearly 1,000 miles of hard riding (had it done so the outer half of the chaincase would have had to be removed for access to the adjustable slipper). But the fact that the

exposed rear chain needed resetting by only one notch on the snail cams in the same period (and 300 miles were covered in rain) speaks well for the rubber cush-drive in the rear hub.

For the most part the whole machine remained admirably oiltight; but towards the end of the test oil began to leak from the cast-in pushrod tunnels (where they cross the cylinder-head join face) and from the front-fork filler screws. A more serious leak from the timing cover was cured by replacing three fixing screws which had vibrated out. The only blemish remaining on the Constellation after a few minutes' cleaning was some blueing of the siamezed exhaust pipes. But it is only fair to add that the machine had done some 4,000 miles of high-speed hack work with precious little attention.

Finished in black and polychromatic blue, with chromium-plated front mudguard and tank sides, the Constellation looks the part—a massive, lovable mile-gobbler.

Specification

ENGINE: Royal Enfield 692 c.c. (70 x 90mm) overhead-valve parallel twin. Crankshaft supported in ball bearing on drive side and roller bearing on timing side; steel-backed white-metal big-end bearings. Separate light-alloy cylinder heads; compression ratio, 8 to 1. Dry-sump lubrication; 4-pint oil tank cast integrally with crankcase.
CARBURETTORS: Two Amal Monoblocs fed from float chamber on left-side instrument. Air slides operated by handlebar lever.
IGNITION and LIGHTING: Lucas magneto with manual timing control. Lucas RM15 alternator, with rotor on left end of crankshaft, charging six-volt, 9-amp-hour battery through rectifier. Lucas 7in-diameter headlamp with pre-focus light unit.
TRANSMISSION: Royal Enfield four-speed gear box bolted to rear of crankcase. Gear ratios: bottom, 12.35 to 1; second, 8.19 to 1; third, 6.05 to 1; top, 4.44 to 1. Multi-plate clutch with cork-base friction facings running in oil. Primary chain, ⅜in duplex in cast-aluminium oil-bath case. Rear chain, ⅝ x ⅜in with guard over top run. Engine r.p.m. at 30 m.p.h. in top gear, 1,700.
FUEL CAPACITY: 4¼ gallons.
TYRES: Dunlop: front 3.25 x 19in ribbed; rear 3.50 x 19in Universal.
BRAKES: 6in-diameter dual front, 7in-diameter single rear; finger adjusters.
SUSPENSION: Royal Enfield telescopic front fork with hydraulic damping. Pivoted rear fork controlled by Armstrong spring-and-hydraulic units with two-position manual adjustment for load.
WHEELBASE: 54in unladen. Ground clearance, 6in unladen.
SEAT: Royal Enfield dual-seat; unladen height, 31in.
WEIGHT: 427 lb fully equipped, with full oil tank and approximately one gallon of petrol.

PRICE: £248 5s 10d; with purchase tax (in Great Britain only), £299 10s.
ROAD TAX: £4 10s a year; £1 13s for four months.
MAKERS: The Enfield Cycle Co., Ltd., Redditch, Worcs.

PERFORMANCE DATA
(Obtained at the Motor Industry Research Association's proving ground at Lindley, Leicestershire.)
MEAN MAXIMUM SPEED: Bottom: *48 m.p.h.
Second: *72 m.p.h.
Third: *98 m.p.h.
Top: 104 m.p.h.
* Valve float occurring.
HIGHEST ONE-WAY SPEED: 106 m.p.h. (conditions: very strong cross wind gusting to 32 m.p.h.; rider lightly clad).

MEAN ACCELERATION:

				10-30 m.p.h.	20-40 m.p.h.	30-50 m.p.h.
Bottom	...	...	...	2.1 sec	1.8 sec	—
Second	...	...	...	2.8 sec	3 sec	2.8 sec
Third	...	...	...	—	4 sec	4.2 sec
Top	...	...	...	—	6.6 sec	6.4 sec

Mean speed at end of quarter-mile from rest: 88 m.p.h.
Mean time to cover standing quarter-mile: 15 sec.
PETROL CONSUMPTION: At 30 m.p.h., 70 m.p.g.; at 40 m.p.h., 74 m.p.g.; at 50 m.p.h., 75 m.p.g.; at 60 m.p.h., 63 m.p.g.
BRAKING: From 30 m.p.h. to rest, 35ft (surface, dry tarmac).
TURNING CIRCLE: 16ft 9in.
MINIMUM NON-SNATCH SPEED: 20 m.p.h. in top gear on full retard.
WEIGHT PER C.C.: 0.62 lb.

Following pages: one of the most handsome machines of its day, the 1961 692 cc Royal Enfield Constellation (*National Motorcycle Museum*)

Norton Dominator 650SS

Any bike which won Britain's two most prestigious production-machine marathons of the day (in this case, the Bemsee 1000-kilometre and the Thruxton 500-Miles) within a few months of its introduction has just got to be a classic. In fact the Syd Lawton-prepared Norton 650SS, co-ridden by Brian Setchell and Phil Read, very nearly achieved a double-double . . .

The pedigree of the Dominator range of vertical twins can be traced back to the 497 cc Model 7, designed by Bert Hopwood and announced late in 1948. Personally, I was not too impressed with the Model 7; it had plunger springing at the rear and an almost-solid Norton Roadholder telescopic fork, which combined to make a ride on my brother's model down Worcester's ripply and war-neglected Tything something to make one's eyeballs revolve in opposite directions.

Be that as it may, it was not too long before the roadster twins adopted the world-renowned twin-loop Featherbed frame. The 497 cc Dominator 88 was joined by the 597 cc Dominator 99, and by the 1961 season there were standard and de luxe versions in each capacity, the de luxe models having their nether ends draped around with tinware.

Early in 1961, Bracebridge Street began production of yet another twin, this time a 647 cc model reserved for export only and labelled the Norton Manxman. The name was an affront to Excelsior fans, of course, and anyway no 650 cc Norton twin had ever raced in the Isle of Man, but the blame lay with Norton's USA distributors, and not with the manufacturers.

The 650 cc model was put on the home market during September, 1961. There were now *three* models in each capacity, for an SS (super sports) trim had been added to the standard and de luxe versions. The main difference between the models was that the SS bikes used twin carburettors instead of one, and magneto ignition instead of coil ignition.

The new 647 cc models were not just overbored Model 99s. They retained the 68 mm bore of the Dominator 99, but had a new crankcase wherein was a shaft affording a stroke of 89 instead of 82 mm, so providing the 647 mm capacity. With the shaft came a wider flywheel, and larger-diameter ($1\frac{3}{4}$-in)

crankpins. The light-alloy cylinder head was derived from that of the works Domiracer, and featured wide-splayed exhaust ports, and parallel inlet tracts. In Dominator 650SS form, the engine had twin $1\frac{1}{16}$-in choke Amal Monobloc carburettors, and developed 49 bhp at 6,800 rpm.

A flat and rather short handlebar was supplied, and the specification included a 150 mph speedometer, but there were various optional extras to be had, embracing a rev-meter, folding kick-start, siamese exhaust pipes, chromium-plated mudguards, and a fully-enclosed rear chain—the latter a rather odd option for what was essentially a production-machine racing model. Unlike the standard and de luxe versions, the 650SS had the traditional Norton finish of black frame and silver tank.

By May, 1962, Nortons had added rearset rests complete with brake and gear levers and gear linkage (at £9 16s 7d, tax included) to the catalogue, and within weeks the first race-equipped 650SS models were in action at Silverstone in the Bemsee 1000-kilometre race. During the practice period, Phil Read had flung the Lawton Norton into a muddy field, but it seemed little the worse for its adventure. As the race got going in rain and high winds, so another 650SS, shared by Ron Langston and Bruce Main-Smith built up a useful lead over the Read/Setchell model in second place, but the Langston/Main-Smith effort ended when the Norton's con-rod made a departure, through the crankcase. From then on, Read and Setchell were never headed.

A month later, the same two machines were engaged in battle at the Thruxton 500-Miles, but this time Read and Setchell led throughout apart from a brief moment or two of glory for Langston and Main-Smith, who eventually had to settle for fifth place after Bruce had rammed the straw bales at the chicane.

Not even the boost to 647 cc could satisfy the power-hungry

Cotswold farmer and motor cycling all-rounder, Ron Langston sweeps his six-fifty Norton past John Griffiths' similar mount, in the 1962 Thruxton 500-mile marathon

Americans, and already Nortons had a still bigger twin under way for export only. This was the 745 cc Atlas, giving the same maximum power output as the 650SS, but possessing a lot more low-down torque. But that was not the only news from Bracebridge Street. The AMC group, in financial trouble, was consolidating and by the end of the year Norton production in Birmingham ended and the famous Bracebridge Street factory was put up for sale.

The last bikes to emerge from the historic premises were 85 Dominator 650SS models ordered by the Queensland Police, for escort duties in connection with the forthcoming visit of Her Majesty the Queen and Prince Philip, to Australia.

Tools and dies having been transferred to Woolwich, production of the Norton twins restarted, and soon there were whispers that nothing fitted properly! Of course not; the Londoners were trying to make parts according to drawing, whereas everybody in Birmingham knew that Old Bill, or Old Fred had ignored the drawings for years and made the bits and pieces by instinct.

The Norton range was much abbreviated for 1963. Not only had the 597 cc Dominator 99 been dropped, but the de luxe Dominator 650 had gone, too, leaving just the standard and SS versions. By May, the 497 cc Dominator 88 de luxe had disappeared, too, and thenceforth there would be no more tail-faired Dommies.

May, too, meant it was time once again for the Bemsee 1000-Kilometre race, the venue for which had been moved from Silverstone to the more interesting circuit of Oulton Park. Again, Phil Read and Brian Setchell took the Lawton Norton into an early lead, but the effort came unstuck when Brian skidded off-course at Druid's Corner. Repairs were affected at

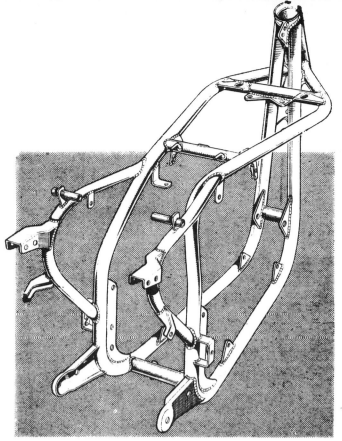

The famous 'featherbed' frame comprised two complete tubular loops which crossed over at the steering head. In the earlier 'wideline' frame the top tubes were parallel. The 'slimline' version was narrowed at the seat nose, for greater comfort and controllability

the pits, but the lost time could not be clawed back, and the pair had to settle for second place, with Langston and Main-Smith third in the class.

Still, Thruxton lay ahead, and honour was restored when Read and Setchell took the chequered flag for the second year running. Indeed, the Lawton Norton was to become almost as famous as a course winner as Slippery Sam, the production TT Triumph, because it was to win for the third time at Thruxton in 1964, although on that occasion Setchell was partnered by Derek Woodman.

By 1964, the only version of the Dominator 650 to be listed was the 650SS. It now had 12-volt electrics, and a steering lock on the front fork. But AMC were rapidly heading for obscurity, and in the next two years there was considerable interchanging of components; for example, Norton Atlas engines were inserted into Matchless frames, Matchless singles into Norton frames, and goodness knows what else. An overhead-camshaft Norton twin had been scuttling around the MIRA test track for some considerable while, but it was destined never to see the production line. From the inevitable collapse, Dennis Poore and his new Norton-Villiers concern rescued the 745 cc Atlas engine (which was really the 650SS bottom end married to a 73-mm bore cylinder block). In due course it would be inclined forward, put into a frame with an Isolastic engine mounting system, and given yet another new name—the Norton Commando. But what happened after that is a tale for later in this book.

Useful note for restorers—The official tank colour of the Dominator 650SS was Norton Quicksilver, but in case this is unobtainable the Norton Owners Club recommends Ford Silver Fox as a substitute.

All Norton twins, from the first 500 cc Dominator up to and including the 850 cc electric-start Norton Commando of the 1970s, were derived from Bert Hopwood's original design featuring a chain-driven front-mounted single camshaft. This is the 1958 597 cc version, with crankshaft-mounted alternator

Following pages: 1964 Norton Dominator 650SS fitted with 12-volt electrics, but generally akin to the 1962 road test version (*National Motorcycle Museum*)

Road Tests of New Models

NORTON DOMINATOR 650 SS

Above: A strong candidate for marathon-race honours, the Dominator 650 SS combines race-bred handling with a power output of 49 b.h.p. There is considerable potential for further development, too, for the inlet tracts can be opened up to 1⅛in by removing sleeves. Below is the handlebar-control and instrument layout

Latest and largest

WORSHIPPERS of high performance must be blessing the growth in popularity of production-machine racing. Since the marathon series—led by the Southampton Club's 500-miler—gained a foothold in the sporting calendar, compression ratios and carburettor choke sizes have climbed; cam contours have become more purposeful and, on many a twin, carburettors have doubled up.

In short, super-sports roadsters have acquired speed and acceleration comparable with those of the production racers of not so long ago; and, where necessary, transmission, braking and suspension have been improved to suit.

As fine an example of the trend as any, and better than most, is Norton's ace sportster and marathon racer—the Dominator 650 Sports Special. Though Nortons were the last to push the capacity of their vertical twins beyond the 600 c.c. mark, they have obviously used the time to good advantage. A mean top speed of 111 m.p.h. and a fastest timed run of 118 m.p.h. speak for themselves.

Indeed, considering the tester was wearing a one-piece waterproof riding suit on top of winter muffling, and that the day was wet and windy with gusts of 25 to 30 m.p.h., those figures do more than speak—they shout. There is little doubt that close-fitting leathers, the rear-set footrests allowed for marathon racing and kinder weather would boost top speed by 3 or 4 m.p.h.

Though some features of the engine reflect the influence of the racing five-hundred twin that Tom Phillis rode into

The carburettor downdraught of 20 degrees is apparent here. Ports and cylinder heads are polished and the sports cams actuate flat-base followers

in famous range approaches two miles a minute yet eats out of your hand

third place in last year's Senior T.T., there is nothing freakish about the Dominator 650 SS. Its high performance stems from sound, straightforward development. As a result the machine is pleasantly tractable even for town work (thanks in part to the use of auto-advance for the magneto and a balance pipe connecting the two induction tracts); and it cannot be faulted for exhaust noise. Provided super-premium petrol is used, the engine is free from pinking; and no great effort is needed to swing it over compression for starting.

By parallel-twin standards the engine is smoother than average. Up to the stipulated r.p.m. limit (6,800) vibration never bothered the rider, although at peak revs it caused the petrol tap to shut off until the cork-sleeved plunger was renewed. Responsible for this comparative smoothness is the extra-stiff crankshaft. Though it is basically similar to the smaller Dominator crankshafts, the crank throw is 3½ mm longer to give the greater stroke of 89 mm (at 68 mm, cylinder bore is the same as on the six-hundred); the flywheel is wider and so more effective; and, most important, crankpin diameter is increased to 1⅜in, making the assembly more rigid.

An optional extra, a chronometric rev-meter was fitted to the test machine. With the needle around the 2,000 to 3,000 r.p.m. sector the Norton might have been any first-class six-fifty. At 4,000 r.p.m. there were indications that the engine was something out of the ordinary. By the time the pointer had swung round to the 5,000 r.p.m. mark the engine was well and truly in the groove; and from there on there was a plain challenge to all comers. Cruising at a speedometer 90 to 95 m.p.h.

(true speed approximately 5 per cent less) was something the Norton was ready to do at the slightest opportunity and happy to sustain indefinitely; there was a comfortable 5,000-odd r.p.m. on the rev-meter and plenty of throttle in hand. Indeed, with the rider normally seated, the timed mean maximum speed proved to be 99 m.p.h. (a ton in normal weather for sure) with a best run of 108 m.p.h.

And to reach those speeds, even from rest, required little more than a quarter of a mile. The drill was to notch second at about 45 m.p.h., third at 70 and top as soon as the speedometer showed a ton. Those speeds correspond approximately to the peak-power engine speed of 6,800 r.p.m.; and the reason the makers stipulate that as the limit in the lower gears is that the engine can otherwise over-rev quicker than a chronometric rev-meter can keep pace. There is no performance gain in over-revving, only needless wear, tear and vibration, although two-rate valve springs and hollow, barrel-shape light-alloy push-rods help to keep valve float at bay until well beyond peak revs. (For production-machine racing the more serious contender would probably change to a magnetic rev-meter and change up at 7,000 r.p.m.)

In the context of standing starts, the figures shown in the data panel could have been bettered fractionally had it not been necessary to feed the clutch in at comparatively low r.p.m. to avoid time-wasting wheelspin on the damp surface. Incidentally, the Avon high-hysteresis Grand Prix rear tyre provided above-average adhesion during hard acceleration or fast cornering on wet roads.

Adopted primarily for safety at sustained

There is plenty of finning and air space between the widely splayed exhaust ports

33

three-figure speeds, the tyre brought another benefit. The curved cross-section of its racing-pattern tread added a refinement to the superlative handling for which Dominators are renowned. At low and medium speeds the machine responded sensitively to the slightest banking effort and the balanced front wheel swung into the turn to exactly the right degree. However high the speed, on straight or curve, the steering never showed the least inclination to waver.

As befits a super-sports mount, springing both front and rear was firm and very effectively damped; for the cost of a fairly hard ride on low-speed bumps it ensured great stability at high speeds with no tendency to pitching on undulations.

The flat handlebar resulted in a riding posture that, after several consecutive hours in the saddle, felt slightly cramped but not stupidly so. A rubber band criss-crossed round the twistgrip by a factory tester was a tacit admission of the slipperiness of the plastic sleeve—and most effective in improving grip.

Once they had bedded down the brakes lost their initial slight sponginess and stopped the Sports Special powerfully and smoothly from any speed. Controllability was such that there was no risk of locking a wheel inadvertently, even on wet roads; and there was no loss of efficiency following prolonged riding in heavy rain.

At 20 degrees, the steep downdraught angle of the inlet tracts called for sparing use of the float tickler before starting and for a small but quick tweak of the twistgrip at the end of the kick-starter swing to "catch" the engine. Failure to observe these precautions resulted in an over-rich mixture in the cylinders so that a wide throttle opening was then needed before the engine would start.

Idling was slow but slightly uneven; riders whose everyday mileage includes much town traffic will find it well worth while precisely synchronizing the settings of both throttle cables, throttle stops and pilot air screws to get the cleanest possible tickover and small-throttle getaway.

To cope with the engine's tremendous punch the Dominator clutch has extra-strong springs and five friction plates instead of the usual four. Clutch operation as a result is heavy, though not too heavy for the tough brand of enthusiast for whom the Sports Special is produced. And correct control adjustment is particularly important, for pressure-plate movement is only just sufficient to give complete freedom with the necessary trace of cable backlash.

All gear changes, upward or downward, were clean and positive. With the engine idling slowly, bottom-gear engagement at rest was well-nigh noiseless. And neutral could be found easily from bottom or second while the machine was rolling or immediately it had come to rest.

Lighting was average. In other words, while 80 m.p.h. cruising caused no anxiety after dark on roads with cats-eye reflectors, 60 m.p.h. was as much as felt safe on roads without these aids.

Save that the chaincase outer half must be removed to get at the clutch pressure-plate adjustment, no problems are posed by maintenance. A penny serves to unfasten the dual-seat and so reveal the tool kit. If required, the rear wheel can be removed without disturbing the chain or brake. Incidentally, a change from a falling to a rising rear-brake cam lever means that the finger adjuster on the brake rod is no longer tucked awkwardly behind the left-hand silencer but is really easy to reach.

Finish? A workmanlike black and silver, with chromium plating available for the mudguards at extra cost.

That, then, is the Dominator 650 Sports Special—Norton's answer to the sportsman's prayer. It is a 49 b.h.p. roadster whose quietness, smoothness and lack of fuss makes its speed deceptive; a machine with such superb handling and braking as to make nearly two miles a minute as safe as a stroll in the garden.

SPECIFICATION

ENGINE: *Norton 647 c.c. (68 x 89mm) overhead-valve vertical twin. Crankshaft supported in ball and roller bearings; plain big-end bearings. Light-alloy cylinder head; compression ratio, 8.9 to 1. Dry-sump lubrication; oil-tank capacity, 4½ pints.*

CARBURETTORS: *Two Amal Monoblocs; air slides operated by handlebar lever.*

IGNITION and LIGHTING: *Lucas magneto with auto-advance. Lucas RM19 alternator, with rotor mounted on drive-side crankshaft, charging Lucas 6-volt, 13-amp-hour battery through rectifier. Lucas 7in-diameter headlamp with pre-focus light unit.*

TRANSMISSION: *A.M.C. four-speed foot-change gear box. Gear ratios: bottom, 11.6 to 1; second, 7.57 to 1; third, 5.52 to 1; top, 4.53 to 1. Multi-plate clutch with bonded friction facings running in oil. Primary chain, ½ x 0.305in in pressed-steel oil-bath case. Rear chain, ⅝ x ¼in with guard over top run. Engine r.p.m. at 30 m.p.h. in top gear, 1,750.*

FUEL CAPACITY: *3⅝ gallons.*

TYRES: *Avon: 3.00 x 19in Speedmaster front; 3.50 x 19in Grand Prix rear.*

BRAKES: *8in diameter front, 7in diameter rear, both 1⅛in wide; finger adjusters.*

SUSPENSION: *Norton Roadholder telescopic front fork with hydraulic damping. Pivoted rear fork controlled by Girling spring-and-hydraulic units with three-position adjustment for load.*

WHEELBASE: *55½in unladen. Ground clearance, 5½in unladen.*

SEAT: *Norton dual-seat; unladen height, 31in.*

WEIGHT: *434 lb fully equipped, with full oil tank and approximately one gallon of petrol.*

PRICE: *£255; with purchase tax (in Great Britain only), £311 2s. Extras: Rev-meter, £5 15s (plus £1 5s 3d p.t.); chrome mudguards, £3 5s (p.t., 14s 4d).*

ROAD TAX: *£4 10s a year; £1 13s for four months.*

MAKERS: *Norton Motors, Ltd., Bracebridge Street, Aston, Birmingham, 6.*

DESCRIPTION: The Motor Cycle, 21 September 1961.

To improve idling, a balance pipe joins the two parallel inlet tracts

PERFORMANCE DATA

(Obtained at the Motor Industry Research Association's proving ground at Lindley, Leicestershire.)

MEAN MAXIMUM SPEED: *Bottom: *46 m.p.h.*
*Second: *71 m.p.h.*
*Third: *98 m.p.h.*
Top: 111 m.p.h.
**Equivalent to peak-power engine r.p.m.*

HIGHEST ONE-WAY SPEED: 118 *m.p.h. (conditions: strong three-quarter wind; rider wearing one-piece waterproof oversuit).*

MEAN ACCELERATION:

	10-30 m.p.h.	20-40 m.p.h.	30-50 m.p.h.
Bottom	2 sec	2.2 sec	—
Second	2.8 sec	3.2 sec	3.2 sec
Third	—	4.8 sec	4.8 sec
Top	—	5.8 sec	6.1 sec

Mean speed at end of quarter-mile from rest: 95 m.p.h.
Mean time to cover standing quarter-mile: 14 sec.

PETROL CONSUMPTION: *At 30 m.p.h., 81 m.p.g.; at 40 m.p.h., 72 m.p.g.; at 50 m.p.h., 64 m.p.g.; at 60 m.p.h., 56 m.p.g.*

BRAKING: *From 30 m.p.h. to rest, 29ft (surface, dry concrete).*

TURNING CIRCLE: *15ft 6in.*

MINIMUM NON-SNATCH SPEED: *20 m.p.h. in top gear.*

WEIGHT PER C.C.: *0.67 lb.*

AJS Model 18 Statesman

It was something of an achievement that *The Motor Cycle* was able to carry out a full road test of an AJS of any kind! Right from the close of the Second World War, the Plumstead end of the AMC combine had been antagonistic to the motor cycle press, refusing to supply any models for road-testing (although the other members of the combine—Norton, James, and Francis-Barnett—were always far more accommodating).

Such an attitude must surely have had an adverse effect on home market sales, particularly in the great outback north of Watford where the natives regarded AJS and Matchless as 'foreign', anyway. Still, Plumstead was beginning to see the light as the 1950s ended, and with the new decade came a more co-operative mood.

The Model 18 was the last survivor of the traditional British 500 cc single with separate engine and gearbox. As road-tester Peter Fraser remarks, the machine's ancestry could be traced to pre-war days. Nevertheless, there was no remaining Wolverhampton blood in the line of descent, and the true begetter was the Matchless G80 Clubman of the late 1930s, hairpin valve springs and all; even then, there had been an AJS Model 18 equivalent in the catalogue, but that one had coil valve springs.

Over the years since the return of peace, the Model 18's engine had been the subject of much redesign work, and there would be more to come before Associated Motor Cycles plunged into financial disaster in July of 1966, bringing an end to Model 18 production.

First major engine change came in September, 1957, when the substitution of a Lucas RM15 alternator for the old magneto and direct-current-dynamo electrics had meant a new crankcase assembly and, at the same time, a cast light-alloy primary chaincase in place of the pressed-steel case which (unless the owner knew the secrets of black magic) almost invariably leaked oil. There was a new timing-side cover, too, incorporating a contact-breaker assembly driven from the end of the inlet camshaft.

Oddly enough, the familiar long-stroke dimensions of 82·5 × 93 mm (498 cc) were retained, even though the competitions version of the Model 18, listed as the Model 18CS, had changed to oversquare dimensions of 86 × 85·5 mm (498 cc) as long ago as 1955. The original Burman gearbox was superseded by an AMC unit (and fitted also by Norton) from May, 1956.

In the next two years there were minor titivations, including the option of a two-tone blue and light grey finish instead of traditional black, and the fitting of chromium-plated tank side panels at extra cost.

The next substantial improvement took place in 1960 when the single-downtube cradle frame was replaced by a new duplex frame that was to last the production life of the bike.

On the 1964 Model 18 Statesman standard Girling rear dampers replace the earlier special units. By this time, too, the front forks and wheels are Norton

Mechanically, there was a redesigned cylinder head with hemispherical combustion chamber, and embodying an angled inlet tract to promote gas swirl. The piston was now flat-top, with valve-head cutaways.

As for the company itself, in September 1959 AMC bought the old Indian Sales Corporation of USA, and henceforth (for a few years, anyway) it would be a wholly-owned division of the Plumstead-based group, distributing AJS and Matchless models in America; that did not last long, and by 1962 the USA distribution was in the hands of Joe Berliner, of New Jersey. For some while there had been rumours that the old AMC factory at Plumstead was to be sold for re-development, and this was confirmed by a news item in June, 1961, that AMC were to carry out a phased move to a new single-storey works outside Sheerness. Four months later, this plan was shelved because, said the company, there was a shortage of the required type of labour in the Sheerness area.

The AJS Model 18, meantime, had acquired an improved oil-pump drive with stronger tooth form, and an external circlip at the upper end of the inlet valve guide, for a more positive location in the head.

So far, the dignified AJS appearance of old had been maintained, but 1962 brought huge die-cast-zinc chromium-plated tank badges in the worst tradition of juke-box Gothic, presumably at the behest of Joe Berliner. At the same time, the entire AJS and Matchless ranges, which had muddled along for decades using nothing but model numbers, were given names, the Model 18 becoming the Statesman, for no obvious reason. Not that anybody on this side of the Atlantic ever called it that, naturally.

More practically, the 1962 Model 18 gained a larger battery, a

Adoption of alternator electrics in 1958 brought a change from pressed-steel to a cast-light-alloy primary chaincase, so eliminating a characteristic AJS feature—the permanent oil leak

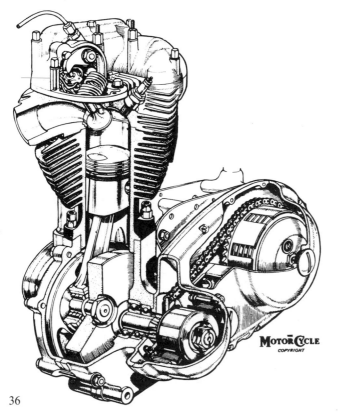

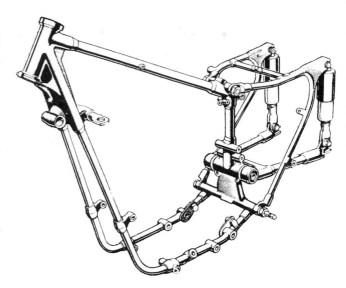

Brazed-lug frame construction, as exemplified by the 1960-onward AJS singles including the Model 18. Steering head and rear fork pivot lugs were malleable-iron castings

more comfortable dual seat, and a better and more insulated method of locating the fuel tank on the frame.

A year later, there were smaller (18-in diameter) wheels, more rounded battery box and oil tank, a fuel tank with knee recesses, and a new full-width hub containing cast light-alloy brake shoes.

The final major change in Model 18 design came in 1964 when a new engine, based on the oversquare Model 18CS unit, was put in hand. The 82·5 mm bore × 93 mm stroke and 497 cc capacity, legacy of the 1930s, was at last discarded in favour of the 86 × 85·5 mm (498 cc) dimensions of the scrambler. The main external change was that the archaic external pushrod tubes were replaced by a cylinder barrel with cast-in pushrod tunnel, the head and barrel being held to the crankcase by through-studs.

Internally, there was a new crankshaft assembly with steel instead of iron flywheels, a double-row-roller big-end bearing with duralumin cage, a roller timing-side main bearing, and totally revised oiling system employing a Norton gear pump instead of the former plunger pump. By this time, of course, AMC had closed the Norton works at Bracebridge Street, Birmingham, and had transferred Norton production to Plumstead, a fact reflected in the use of a Norton Roadholder telescopic front fork instead of the long-in-the-tooth Matchless Teledraulic design.

This should have been the finest Model 18 of all time but, alas, it had insufficient time in which to prove itself. Sinking ever deeper into the mire, AMC were now carrying out a remarkable juggling act, by which Matchless and AJS models found themselves powered by Norton engines in an attempt to find something for Joe Berliner to sell. It was all too late, a hoped-for reconstruction of the group with the aid of USA capital came to nothing and, inevitably, an official receiver was appointed.

There was a 1967 range, announced by Dennis Poore's new and unfamiliar firm of Norton-Matchless Ltd, but it was entirely twin-cylinder, and the Model 18 had gone for good. Under new management, AJS would live again but (oh, horror!) as a *two-stroke*; that rumbling sound heard up in Wolverhampton was A. J. Stevens and his brothers turning in their graves.

ROAD TESTS
OF NEW MODELS

498 c.c. A.J.S. Model 18 Statesman

DISCRETION, dignity and an ability to cope with hard work without showing signs of stress— these are some of the essential attributes of a statesman. Thus when A.J.S. decided to give their machines names in addition to terse designations it was fitting that they should call the 498 c.c. Model 18 the Statesman.

A robust, good-looking roadster single with an ancestry reaching back to well before the last war it can claim, in the motor-cycle sense, to embody all these qualities. The main source of the Statesman's appeal is that it offers a pleasing compromise between the modern and traditional in matters of styling.

Riding the A.J.S. the first few miles reminded one, at a time when vertical twins are fashionable, of the particular charm of the lusty, tractable single. With a maximum in the eighties, the Model 18 is certainly no sluggard. In fact the machine was capable of sustaining 70-75 m.p.h. indefinitely.

In that range the engine was working well within its limit. Hills or headwinds on main roads could be tackled comfortably, the engine pulling hard in top gear. If the occasion demanded that the speed be maintained a quick change into third

was the drill. This ratio (6.13 to 1) proved invaluable when a high average was required especially on hilly, winding roads. Speedy overtaking could be achieved in third—which provided good acceleration between 30 and 70 m.p.h.

At the lower end of the scale the engine would slog like a side-valve. The combination of good flywheel effect, a moderate (7.3 to 1) compression ratio and an efficient auto-advance control made a major contribution to this impression. Indeed, advocates of manual ignition control would find a very hard case to answer. There was no pinking during the test, even when deliberate attempts were made to provoke it. Premium-grade petrol was used throughout.

Possessing all the mechanical quietness which was the hallmark of its predecessors, the Statesman also has an effectively subdued exhaust. Although an air filter is not fitted to the carburettor as standard, induction roar was not obtrusive. This generally low noise level, therefore, plus the fact that there was ample power at low revolutions, enabled the machine to be ridden discreetly in the most congested of urban areas.

Carburation was clean throughout the range. The engine picked up unhesitat-

ingly as soon as the throttle was opened and, once warm, would idle with a steady, reliable beat.

The speedometer read approximately 5 per cent fast, and the instrument would have been easier to read, especially in conditions of poor visibility, had the needle been backed by a black back-

The contact breaker is driven off the inlet camwheel and is readily accessible. Two screws secure the light-alloy cover

Following pages: nobody liked the massive metal tank badges of the Model 18, which is why Ray Bruner's 1965 machine has plain gold transfers (*Bob Currie*)

Robust roadster single, combining good power output and tractability: first-class handling and braking

Orthodox handlebar layout is employed. The switch on the left of the headlamp controls the lights while that on the right is for ignition

This shot emphasizes the trim, workmanlike appearance of the Statesman. The duplex frame has lugs for sidecar attachment

position makes itself known. In this respect the Statesman earned high marks. If any criticism is due, it is that the footrests could with benefit be positioned an inch or so farther to the rear, to relieve the rider's arms from some strain when cruising for long periods in the seventies.

Controls fell readily to hand or foot as the case was. The dual-seat proved very comfortable and generous enough dimensionally to accommodate a passenger without cramping. Fitted as standard, the passenger's footrests had rubbers of the same size as those for the rider and resulted in greater comfort than the usual type. Plastic handlebar grips are fitted. Owing to the nature of the material, and insufficient depth of pattern, the amount of friction they offered, especially during cold or wet conditions, was considered inadequate.

Both front and rear brakes were light in action and could be delicately controlled. During performance tests successive stops from maximum speed

ground (about two-thirds of the needle rotates over a light grey surface). While the performance figures were being obtained the main mileage record jumped 1,000 miles. A trip mileage recorder is fitted, and could easily be reset by means of the knob protruding from the base of the headlamp.

Handling inspired confidence at all times. The machine could be ridden to a standstill in heavy traffic feet-up without undue effort. Steering lock was felt to be rather limited for a model of this nature. The lack of it made manhandling in and out of limited garaging space, a twice-daily task for many ride-to-work enthusiasts, more awkward than was thought desirable. Centre and prop stands are provided. Both were easily operated and gave safe support.

On the open road the Statesman could be ridden to the limit of its performance

without betraying any tendency to deviate from the chosen line. Zestful cornering was encouraged by the way in which the model could, with little effort, be banked from side to side through bends.

Both front and rear springing are hydraulically damped and possessed just that right degree of firmness—an effective compromise between the stiff action needed for stability at high speeds and a soft one for comfort at lower speeds. When the machine was ridden one-up, the three-position Girling units were used in their softest setting. By means of the C-spanner provided in the tool kit they proved quickly adjustable. The Model 18 displayed no tendency to pitching on undulating surfaces and was ridden on unmade, potholed roads without the suspension ever bottoming.

As the miles on a journey mount up so the suitability, or otherwise, of the riding

Adjustment of the clutch thrust rod is simply effected. Removal of a threaded cap exposes the adjuster in the centre of the clutch pressure plate

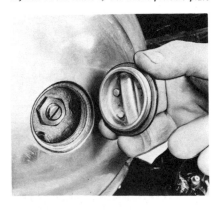

For 1962 a silver-coloured metal motif embellishes the fuel tank of the Statesman

for the generator to balance the full lighting load.

Mounted under the seat, the horn would be more effective if it had a louder and perhaps higher - pitched note. Complete experimental discharging of the battery proved that the emergency-start system was up to its task and that the generator could restore the battery to a useable state of charge after a few miles running.

·Located on the left just below the dual-seat, the roomy tool box could be opened with a coin. The tool kit provided is reasonably comprehensive and contains enough tools for most routine maintenance jobs. A most informative instruction book is also provided. Opening the tool box exposes the battery for inspection. It is held in position by a tensioned rubber strap which has the advantage that, besides being easy to undo, it will not be affected should it become exposed to electrolyte spray. The battery level can be checked with the battery in position.

Removal of two screws allows a light-alloy cover to be detached from the timing chest thus revealing the contact breaker (which is driven by the inlet camwheel).

The Statesman is finished in black relieved by touches of chromium plating. The absence of the familiar A.J.S. gold lining on the fuel tank will be regretted by many enthusiasts. But for those who prefer colour, the model is available in blue with white mudguards.

To sum up, then, the Statesman is a good-looking, well-mannered mount, equally suitable for the daily round or for long week-end runs.

were made without any loss in efficiency or of adjustment.

Starting a big single when overnight temperatures are around freezing point calls for a certain amount of technique. On the Model 18 the drill was to flood the carburettor slightly, close the handlebar-mounted air lever and, with the exhaust-valve lifter in operation, give a long, swinging kick, releasing the lifter when the kick-starter pedal was at the bottom of its travel. In practice the method advised by the makers of easing the engine over compression, releasing the valve lifter and then kicking did not spin the engine sufficiently to start it in severe conditions. It was quite effective enough,

though, as soon as the engine was warm.

Clutch operation was progressive, but on the heavy side. Hard usage during the test caused no loss of adjustment. Gear changes in both directions were both positive and silent. Bottom-gear engagement with the engine idling caused, at worst, no more than a slight click. Neutral could be selected without difficulty.

Lighting was adequate for cruising in the sixties after dark. The dipped beam could be readily selected by an easily accessible switch on the handlebar. The headlamp can be adjusted after slackening the two pivot bolts. The charging rate at 30 m.p.h. in top gear was sufficient

Specification

ENGINE: A.J.S. 498 c.c. (82.5 x 93mm) overhead-valve single. Crankshaft supported in plain and ball bearings; roller big-end bearing. Light-alloy cylinder head; compression ratio 7.3 to 1. Dry-sump lubrication; oil-tank capacity, 4 pints.

CARBURETTOR: Amal Monobloc; air slide operated by handlebar lever.

IGNITION and LIGHTING: Lucas coil ignition with auto-advance. Lucas RM15 alternator with rotor mounted on drive-side crankshaft, charging Lucas 6-volt, 11-amp-hour battery through rectifier. Lucas 7in-diameter headlamp with pre-focus light unit.

TRANSMISSION: A.M.C. four-speed foot-change gear box. Gear ratios: bottom, 12.86 to 1; second, 8.53 to 1; third, 6.13 to 1; top, 5.02 to 1. Multi-plate clutch with bonded friction facings running in oil. Primary chain, ⅜ x 0.305in in light-alloy oil-bath case. Rear chain, ⅝ x ⅜in with guard over top run. Engine r.p.m. at 30 m.p.h. in top gear, 2,000.

FUEL CAPACITY: 4¼ gallons.

TYRES: Dunlop: 3.25 x 19in ribbed front; 3.50 x 19in Universal rear.

BRAKES: 7in-diameter front and rear; finger adjusters.

SUSPENSION: A.M.C. Teledraulic telescopic front fork with hydraulic damping. Pivoted rear fork controlled by Girling spring-and-hydraulic units with three-position adjustment for load.

WHEELBASE: 55½in unladen. Ground clearance, 5½in unladen.

SEAT: A.J.S. dual-seat; unladen height 31in.

WEIGHT: 403 lb fully equipped, with full oil tank and approximately one gallon of petrol.

PRICE: £208 10s; with purchase tax (in Great Britain only), £254 7s 5d Extras: Blue finish with white mudguards, £3 10s (plus 15s 5d p t.); quickly-detachable rear wheel, £2 2s (p.t., 9s 3d).

ROAD TAX: £4 10s a year; £1 13s for four months.

MAKERS: A.J.S. Motor Cycles, Plumstead Road, London, S.E.18.

DESCRIPTION: *The Motor Cycle,* 14 September, 1961.

PERFORMANCE DATA

(Obtained at the Motor Industry Research Association's proving ground at Lindley, Leicestershire.)

MEAN MAXIMUM SPEED: Bottom: 38 m.p.h.*
Second: 57 m.p.h.*
Third: 77 m.p.h.
Top: 82 m.p.h.
*Valve float occuring.

HIGHEST ONE-WAY SPEED: 87 m.p.h. (conditions: strong following wind; rider wearing two-piece suit and overboots).

MEAN ACCELERATION:

	10-30 m.p.h.	20-40 m.p.h.	30-50 m.p.h.
Bottom:	3.6 sec.		
Second	4.8 sec	4.4 sec	4.6 sec
Third:	—	7 sec	5.8 sec
Top:	—	9.2 sec	8.6 sec

Mean speed at end of quarter-mile from rest: 68 m.p.h.
Mean time to cover standing quarter-mile: 18.4 sec.

PETROL CONSUMPTION: At 30 m.p.h., 84 m.p.g.; at 40 m.p.h., 72 m.p.g.; at 50 m.p.h., 64 m.p.g.; at 60 m.p.h., 52 m.p.g.

BRAKING: From 30 m.p.h. to rest. 29ft 6in (surface, dry tarmac).

TURNING CIRCLE: 16ft.

MINIMUM NON-SNATCH SPEED: 20 m.p.h. in top gear.

WEIGHT PER C.C.: 0.81 lb.

Ariel Sports Arrow

Ariel general manager Ken Whistance and his happy crew at the Selly Oak works in Birmingham went right out on a limb when tooling-up for quantity production of Val Page's imaginative 249 cc two-stroke-twin Leader. The construction of the machine entailed a complete breakaway from anything ever before built at the factory, for it relied intensively on steel pressings, with the major item an immensely strong hollow beam (formed from two edge-welded pressings) from which the engine-gear unit was suspended. Dies to produce pressings that big were rather costly.

To recoup the outlay, the Leader just *had* to sell. But regrettably, although the public at large were content to admire from a distance, they were slow in coming forward to buy. However, the Leader was by no means a flop (in fact, the Selly Oak people threw a party to celebrate the 25,000th Leader to come off the assembly line) but it was no sales record-buster, either.

The Leader was conceived as a super-tourer, with built-in everything from engine enclosure, legshields and handlebar screen, to rear carrier and metal pannier boxes. This was fine, except that the specification was far too staid for ebullient youth. To cater for the young rider, something rather more sporty, perhaps, was needed, yet making use of the pressings produced from those expensive dies.

As Val Page was on the point of retiring from work,

development of a derived model more acceptable to the younger element was passed to Bernard Knight. He discarded the Leader's superstructure and enclosure, and started again from the front fork, frame beam, and engine unit. A rather smaller dummy 'tank' pressing was devised (the real fuel tank, as on the Leader, was within the frame beam, with the filler cap under the termite-proof plywood base of the seat), with ears projecting forward of the steering head to carry the headlamp.

A tool box was sunk into the top face of the dummy tank, and removal of the tool box gave access to parcel space (and to the tyre pump). A neat touch was that access to the rectifier was gained by removing the left-side tank badge and so disclosing an aperture.

Careful use of two-tone paintwork produced a machine which was still unorthodox in appearance, yet looked lighter and nippier than the Leader. Nor was it just a matter of looks. It really *was* lighter, by almost 50 lb, and since the engine was the same for both models, the loss of weight resulted in a rather better performance.

This, then, was the Arrow, launched in December, 1959. It sold well in Britain, if not abroad, and it was adopted for beat patrol work by some urban police forces. What was rather less expected was that the road-racing boys should see in the Arrow a potential racer. Nevertheless, it was an Arrow tuned by

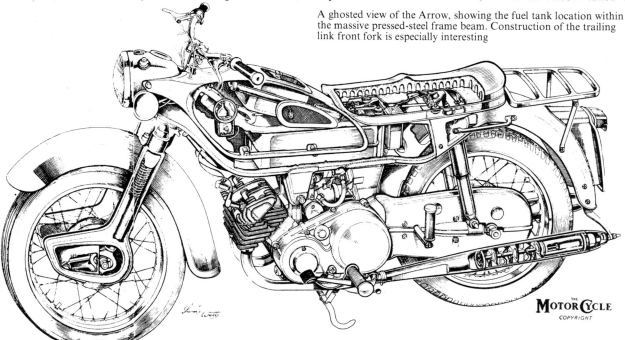

A ghosted view of the Arrow, showing the fuel tank location within the massive pressed-steel frame beam. Construction of the trailing link front fork is especially interesting

Hermann Meier and ridden by Mike O'Rourke that gave Britain its best 250 cc TT placing for many a long year, by finishing seventh (at an average speed of 80·18 mph) in the 1960 event, right astern of Taniguchi's works Honda.

In the months ahead, others (notably Peter Inchley and Maurice Spalding) followed O'Rourke's example and brought Ariel Arrows to the race-circuit starting grids.

In a very different field, trials ace Sammy Miller (accompanied by Jeff Smith on a C15T BSA) took an Arrow up Ben Nevis until deep snowdrifts barred further upward progress. For the record, Sammy had substituted a 20-in front wheel, for better ground clearance, and had lowered the gearing overall until bottom ratio was something like 30 to 1.

Aided and abetted by Ariel development engineer Clive Bennett, the old firm of Ernie Earles and Bill Boddice concocted a *four-cylinder* Ariel Arrow racing sidecar outfit, and it was intended that Ron Langston should drive it in the 1962 Sidecar TT. It got as far as the Isle of Man, but the device coupling the two Arrow engines came adrift as Ron was being pushed away for his first practice lap. After a rebuild he tried again, only to suffer a broken connecting rod.

So, the double-Arrow was a non-starter. But unknown to the public it was also a mobile test-bed for the Lucas company's experiments in electronic ignition, and if only for that reason it deserves a place in history.

The Leader had been voted Machine of the Year in 1959, and the Arrow took the same title for 1960. With the announcement in January, 1961, of yet another variant on the twin-two-stroke theme, it seemed that Ariels were bidding fair to make it three-in-a-row.

The newcomer was, of course, the Sports Arrow—quickly nicknamed the Golden Arrow because of the gilded finish of its dummy tank and rear number plate pressing. At first, the gold was combined with light battleship grey for the remaining parts of the model, but this later became a richer ivory.

To add yet more glamour, there were whitewall tyres, semi-dropped handlebars, and chromium-plated covers for the timing side and the front fork legs, while a small perspex sports handlebar screen completed the picture. To justify the 'Super Sports' tag, a $1\frac{1}{16}$-in bore Amal Monobloc carburettor was

Ariel experimental chief Clive Bennett works with Ernie Handley (*left*) and Ernie Earles on the unique four-cylinder Ariel Arrow which Ron Langston was to have raced in the 1962 Sidecar TT. The power band was too narrow

employed instead of the $\frac{7}{8}$-in Monobloc of the standard Arrow.

The model was possessed of abundant energy, and on a Golden Arrow borrowed from the Selly Oak development department for an hour or two, I was able to climb the long slope to the Wyche Cutting (the gap through the ridge of Worcestershire's Malvern Hills) in third gear and on half throttle. To anyone who knows the area, that was a pretty convincing demonstration.

The power output of the Golden Arrow was 20 bhp at 6,650 rpm, and it retained this figure throughout its production run. By the beginning of 1963, motor cycle sales as a whole were plunging, and the BSA Group's decision to close Selly Oak and transfer Leader and Arrow production to the main Small Heath works was no doubt justified.

It has been said that at the time of the closure, Ariel's order book stood at only 15 machines. One snag was that certain overseas markets, including the USA, did not like the idea of a pressed-steel frame (which was illogical, since they happily accepted Honda and Suzuki lightweights, of very similar construction). To overcome the objection, development of a tubular-framed Arrow was put in hand, and the two prototypes covered quite a respectable test mileage.

Alas, there never was a production tubular-frame Arrow, and the reason was that Burman, the gearing manufacturers who provided the internals for the Leader/Arrow box, were now so deeply involved in the production of car steering mechanisms for Austin-Morris that they wanted to take their leave of the motor cycle field. To bridge the gap, BSA explored the possibility of filling the Arrow gearbox shell with C15 internals, but it could not be done without considerable redesign of the complicated Ariel crankcase-gearbox casting. With overall sales so low, this was not possible.

To use up Ariel frame pressings, a 199 cc budget version of the Arrow was announced early in 1964 (the bait was that the purchaser paid a cheaper 'Under-200 cc' insurance rate) but by then the end was already in sight, for production of the Leader and all three versions of the Arrow stopped in 1965.

'I shot an Arrow in the air . . .' In March, 1961, trials ace Sammy Miller (Ariel Arrow) and moto-cross champion Jeff Smith (BSA) tried a motor cycle climb of Ben Nevis. Deep snow near the summit frustrated their efforts.

ROAD TESTS OF CURRENT MODELS

Above: Tools and inflator are carried in a compartment in the dummy tank. Right: Sleek and cobby—and glamorous—the Sports Arrow looks every inch a thoroughbred

Below: First steps in front-wheel removal are to take off the chromium-plated covers at the base of the fork legs and to insert the special tools through the holes provided and into the links. Bottom: Fuel filler and battery are revealed by raising the hinged dual-seat

247 c.c. Ariel Sports Arrow

HIGH-PERFORMANCE TWIN WITH SUPERB HANDLING

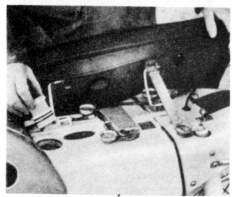

IT is not so very long ago that Ariels, renowned for their range of four-strokes, took a bold and somewhat unexpected step. Casting their established models—including the illustrious Square Four—on the scrapheap they staked their all on the success of an unconventional two-stroke twin; it was, of course, the lavishly-equipped Leader two-fifty. The gamble paid off, and soon there was a second version of the same basic design in the lively but low-cost Arrow. And that, too, hit the jackpot.

Could Ariels do it yet again? Indeed they could, for just over a year ago a third variation of the theme was revealed. Gaily finished with gold-enamelled tank shell and rear-number-plate pressing, it was the Sports Arrow. Chromium plating brightened the front-fork cover plates, tool-box lid and right-hand engine cover. White-wall tyres were specified at front and rear. The cast, light-alloy primary chaincase was highly polished. An abbreviated flyscreen graced the rakish, low-level handlebar. Control levers were of ball-end pattern.

Nor was the beauty merely skin deep. This was a true sports mount, fitted with a larger-diameter carburettor than the roadster model, and with corresponding modifications to the cylinder-wall porting which boosted the power output to a healthy 20 b.h.p. at 6,500 r.p.m. As tested in its 1962 guise, the machine appears even more glamorous, for now the gilded tank shell is allied to an ivory finish for the frame, forks and mudguards, so producing almost a "Regency" effect.

And what of the overall impression of the Sports Arrow? Favourable, most favourable. Speed the test machine produced, and then some, but the charm lay in the manner in which the model produced its performance. Its range-mates, the Leader and Arrow, had already achieved a reputation for rock-steady steering and this attribute is, of course, equally applicable to the sports version. Normally, a tuned two-stroke can be a thirsty little beast but the Ariel turned out to be surprisingly light on fuel and, in give-and-take going throughout the test, produced an average figure of about 70 m.p.g.

However, there were also one or two points to be noted on the debit side of the ledger. Starting from cold, for instance, usually called for a dozen or so prods of the

Specification

ENGINE: Ariel 247 c.c. (54 x 54mm) two-stroke twin. Separate iron cylinders and light-alloy heads. Roller big-end bearings. Crankshaft supported in three ball bearings. Compression ratio, 10 to 1. Petroil lubrication; mixture ratio, 20 to 1 (except Shell 2T or B.P. Zoom, 25 to 1).
CARBURETTOR: Amal Monobloc with 1$\frac{1}{16}$in choke. Rod-operated strangler. Mesh-type air filter.
TRANSMISSION: Four-speed, foot-change gear box in unit with engine. Ratios: bottom, 19 to 1; second, 11 to 1; third, 7.8 to 1; top, 5.9 to 1. Three-plate clutch operating in oil. Primary chain $\frac{3}{8}$ x 0.225in in oil-bath case; rear chain $\frac{1}{2}$ x 0.305in, in pressed-steel case. Engine r.p.m. at 30 m.p.h. in top gear, 2,600.
IGNITION and LIGHTING: Lucas 50-watt RM18 alternator. Coil ignition. Lucas 13-ampere-hour battery. 6in-diameter headlamp with 30/24-watt main bulb.
FUEL CAPACITY: 3 gallons, including reserve.
TYRES: Dunlop 3.25 x 16in whitewall; studded rear, ribbed front.
BRAKES: 6in diameter x 1$\frac{1}{8}$in wide, front and rear.
SUSPENSION: Ariel trailing-link front fork, hydraulically damped Pivoted rear fork controlled by two Armstrong spring and hydraulic units.
WHEELBASE: 51in unladen. Ground clearance, 5in, unladen. Seat height, 28$\frac{1}{2}$in unladen.
WEIGHT: 305 lb, including approximately one gallon of petroil.
PRICE: £190 15s 7d, including British purchase tax.
ROAD TAX: £2 5s a year.
MAKERS: Ariel Motors Ltd , Grange Road, Selly Oak, Birmingham, 29.
DESCRIPTION: The Motor Cycle, 19 January 1961.

Perform:nce Data

(Obtained at the Motor Industry Research Association's proving ground, Lindley, Leicestershire.)

MEAN MAXIMUM SPEED: Bottom: 30 m.p.h.
Second: 49 m.p.h.
Third: 64 m.p.h.
Top: 78 m.p.h.

HIGHEST ONE-WAY SPEED: 81 m.p.h. (conditions: light three-quarter breeze, 10-stone rider wearing helmet, riding boots and two-piece trials suit).

MEAN ACCELERATION:

	10–30 m.p.h.	20–40 m.p.h.	30–50 m.p.h.
Bottom	2.1 sec	—	—
Second	3.9 sec	4.5 sec	—
Third	—	8.0 sec	7.7 sec
Top	—	15.4 sec	13.2 sec

Mean speed at end of quarter-mile from rest: 70 m.p.h. Mean time to cover standing quarter-mile: 17.6 sec.
PETROIL CONSUMPTION: At 30 m.p.h., 108 m.p.g.; at 40 m.p.h. 82 m.p.g.; at 50 m.p.h., 74 m.p.g.; at 60 m.p.h., 56 m.p.g.
BRAKING: From 30 m.p.h. to rest, 30ft (surface, dry asphalt).
TURNING CIRCLE: 12ft 10in.
MINIMUM NON-SNATCH SPEED: 18 m.p.h. in top gear.
WEIGHT PER C.C.: 1.23 lb.

pedal with the strangler fully closed. Once the engine was warm a first-kick start could be guaranteed. Then there was the riding position. A down-turned handlebar is certainly not to everyone's taste though, admittedly, it is traditionally a part of a sports-machine specification; but here the footrests are in a normal, forward position and, if full use is to be made of the dropped bar, the resulting crouch is not the most comfortable. As for the flyscreen, while this may have its advantages when a rider is well tucked down, for normal riding it is little more than ornamental and, indeed, tends to obscure part of the speedometer dial.

The acceleration of the Ariel, as reference to the data panel will show, was pretty fantastic for a two-fifty. The standing quarter-mile in 17.6s.? That is as good as, if not better than, the average five-hundred—nor was it a fluke reading, for the figure was the average of several runs. One conclusion which could be drawn is that the engine possesses an unusually wide power band; and that was borne out by the road performance.

With most sports two-strokes the power is concentrated at the upper end of the rev scale and, after a slow build-up, comes in almost as though the rider has been kicked in the rear. With the Sports Arrow the power build-up is more evenly spread and, as a result, there is less need to recourse to the lower gear ratios.

In illustration of this, it was quite possible to allow the machine to accelerate steadily from speeds as low as 25 m.p.h. in top though, of course, a drop into third produced a much zippier getaway. Furthermore, where time was not pressing, long, main-road hills could be climbed with top gear still engaged.

When main-road conditions allowed, many miles were covered with the speedometer needle varying between 60 and 65 m.p.h. (an electronic test proved the dial 6 per cent optimistic). Even at 60 there was plenty of urge still to come should the need arise.

Ariel steering is already a byword, and so utterly safe did the Sports Arrow feel that there was the greatest possible fun to be had from flinging the model through a twisty section of road. A further safety factor is the performance of the 6in-diameter brakes at front and rear, and the quoted figure of 30ft from 30 m.p.h. is

genuine enough. Nor are the stoppers in any way "sudden," for the machine comes to a halt smoothly and progressively.

The gear-change pedal has a light, if somewhat long movement, and ratios could be located readily. Noiseless changes, upward or downward, were child's play, although the change was found to be unusually sensitive to primary and rear-chain adjustment.

In town areas the large-capacity twin silencers earned high marks for the exhaust's quiet, droning song. When the taps were opened wide, or when the Ariel was accelerated hard, the song changed to a deeper, louder tune but this was always of an acceptable standard. Mechanical noise from the engine and transmission was at a commendably low level. An annoying clatter from below was traced to a bouncing centre stand; a change of stand spring brought little improvement. Another source of annoyance was the tool box, inset in the upper face of the "tank" pressing; access to the box itself was simple enough, but to extract the tyre pump the tool tray, held in place by a spring cross-bar, had first to be removed—and replacement of the bar was something of a fiddle. However, this small point was far outweighed by the many practical features of the model.

Handling? Absolutely top-line—in fact there's many a racing machine which uses the standard Arrow beam and front fork. Suspension? Top-line again; one-up or two-up, the Sports Arrow floats over the bumpy surfaces. Speed? Near-80, if you want it; day-long cruising in the sixties, if you wish.

Following pages: the Sports Arrow was usually called the Golden Arrow, from its tank finish. Shown here is a 1963 version (*National Motorcycle Museum*)

BSA Rocket Gold Star

Even the most rabid BSA enthusiast will have to admit that at various times in the firm's history, Small Heath gave birth to thorough stinkers—the 1921 Senior TT models, the 1928 175 cc two-stroke, and so on up to and including the Ariel Three tricycle moped. Yet between times some highly covetable models trundled down Armoury Road, and one of these was the Rocket Gold Star.

In a sense, the Rocket Goldie was already obsolete when it was first announced in February, 1962. It was the last of the pre-unit twins, essentially a marriage of the well-tried A10 Super Rocket engine with a modified single-cylinder Gold Star frame, and because BSA had already begun production of their A50 and A65 unit-construction twins this was just a handy way of using up surplus stocks of parts. Once the supply of pre-unit engines had dried up, there would be no more Rocket Goldies, which explains why the model was only listed in 1962 and 1963.

Nevertheless it was a very handsome machine, and so sought-after nowadays that fake Rocket Gold Stars are making an appearance. Beware, you would-be buyers, especially at auction sales. A favourite dodge is to instal an A10 engine in a single-cylinder BSA frame, and here the immediate give-away is the bulge in the right-hand cradle tube (which, on a single, is necessary to clear the oil-pump housing). It should also be noted that in 1962, Rocket Goldie engine numbers ran from DA10R.5958 onward, and frame numbers from GA10.101 onward. The corresponding 1963 identifications are engine numbers from DA10R.8197 onward, and frame numbers from GA10.390 onward. The same engine number sequences cover Super Rocket and Spitfire models also, but *only* the Rocket Gold Star used GA10-series frames.

The only major difference from the light alloy-head Super Rocket engine was a compression ratio of 9 to 1, instead of 8·25 to 1. Ignition was by magneto with manual advance/retard

On clubman-type racing machines torque characteristics are a compromise between touring and racing requirements. Here is Maurice Spalding on a BSA Rocket Gold Star in the 1962 Thruxton 500-miler

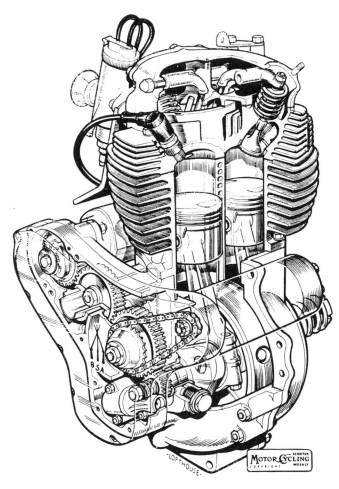

The 1960 646 cc BSA Super Rocket engine which, when housed in a basically Gold Star frame, produced the much-coveted Rocket Gold Star. It was the final development of the pre-unit BSA twin

lever, a direct-current dynamo looked after the electric supply, and the exhaust system embraced siamese pipes and a single, Gold Star-type silencer on the right.

The front fork and wheel were pure Goldie, and since the twin was intended for clubman racing it featured a quickly-detachable headlamp with plug-and-socket wiring harness connection, reversible handlebar, and an exceptionally close-ratio gearbox (overall figures were 4·52, 4·96, 5·96 and 7·92 initially, although this was perhaps a mite *too* close, and for the following year they were widened slightly, as indicated in the specification panel).

There was also a list of racing goodies available, including light-alloy wheel rims, rear-set footrests, clip-on bars and a 'track silencer'. In roadgoing trim, power output of the engine was 46 bhp at 6,250 rpm, but with modest tuning this could be pushed up to 50 bhp.

The Rocket Gold Star did not do much production-machine racing. One example, shared by David Dixon and Maurice Spalding, and prepared by Syd Lawton, failed to distinguish itself in the 1962 Silverstone 1000 and Thruxton 500; it did finish, but well down the field—at Silverstone, with a serious oil leak and a loss of power ten laps from the end, which meant very careful nursing until the chequered flag went out.

Three Rocket Gold Stars contested the 1963 Thruxton marathon, with the machine shared by Ron Langston and Dave Williams tipped to have the best chance. Unluckily, the lap-scorers credited them with a lap too few in the early stages, but once the correction was made it was seen that they were up in a creditable third place. But later in the race an oil union fractured, and much time was lost at the pits in effecting a repair. Then it was 'on with the race', and Ron and Dave did well to work their way back to sixth place in the multi-cylinder class by the end.

The model was officially out of production by the time of the 1964 Thruxton 500 (although in fact the factory records show that 12 more were built after August, 1963). Again the same three pairs of riders rode the same three Rocket Goldies, but this time there was to be no joy in the BSA camp. Ron Langston and Dave Williams were out after no more than 22 laps, as the result of a blown cylinder head joint; R. Mahan and G. Smith followed six laps later with gearbox problems, while D. Face and E. Denyer lasted for 125 laps before making their exit with faulty ignition. Ironically, it was around this time that production-machine racing began to get into its stride internationally, but effectively the Rocket Gold Star was no longer around.

Finally, here are a few notes for restorers of the model, by courtesy of Colin Wall. Correct mudguards for the Rocket Gold Star are rather difficult to find. They are identified by a beaded flare on the leading edge of the front guard, and the trailing edge of the rear guard—they are *neither* single-cylinder Gold Star type, *nor* A65 Lightning pattern. There should be six separate stays to the front guard.

The rear registration plate is of the open-sided type, not the boxed-in plate mounting of the roadster twins, and is identical to that used on the mid-1950 Bantams. The dual seat is the same as that of the A10 of the early 1960s, but the rev-meter is driven at a 3 to 1 ratio, and is of a type used exclusively on the Rocket Gold Star and Super Rocket.

It was a favourite habit of Rocket Gold Star owners of the day to replace the standard four-gallon steel tank with a glass-fibre or light-alloy unit, as fashion dictated. Nevertheless, the bike looks far better when fitted with the original tank. This should have chromium-plated side panels outlined in maroon (not red). The rest of the tank is finished in silver, and for a good match Colin recommends Volkswagen Beetle silver.

A BSA Rocket Gold Star comes in for awed scrutiny at the 1962 Earls Court Show. It was carrying about £60-worth of optional extras

Following pages: last of the BSA separate-engine vertical twins was the 650 cc Rocket Gold Star of 1962-3 (*National Motorcycle Museum*)

ROAD TESTS OF NEW MODELS

646 c.c. B.S.A. Rocket

Scintillating high-performance road burner: good brakes, excellent rider comfort and docile traffic manners

AN 85 m.p.h. top-gear spread speaks volumes for the tractability of a sporting engine. And on top of this the 646 c.c. B.S.A. Rocket Gold Star has effortless, surging acceleration through the gears and a tireless 90 m.p.h. cruising gait. The maximum of 105 m.p.h. obtained on test could certainly have been bettered had the November weather been co-operative.

The standard Super Rocket engine, with compression ratio raised from 8.25 to 9 to 1, is housed in a Gold Star frame. Narrow, chromium-plated mudguards, four-gallon petrol tank with snap filler, rubber gaiters and chromed dust covers on the front fork and matching speedometer and rev-meter are inherited from the Gold Star.

For production-machine racing, the full range of Gold Star extras and a track silencer, said to boost power output by 4 b.h.p., are available.

Although most of its contemporary rivals boast twin carburettors for maximum performance, the Rocket Gold Star has a single Amal Monobloc.

This is perhaps one of the prime factors in the sweetness of carburation at the lower end of the scale.

From tickover at 800 r.p.m., the engine answered the throttle crisply and instantaneously, provided the ignition lever was used intelligently. From 1,500 r.p.m., beefy, usable power was on tap right up to the manufacturers' recommended ceiling of 6,800 r.p.m., at which 46 b.h.p. is developed.

CLOSE RATIOS

Gold Star close-ratio gears are employed; a bottom ratio of 8.39 to 1 necessitated slipping the clutch to prevent the r.p.m. dropping below 1,500. Above 15 m.p.h., the clutch could be ignored and the ignition lever gradually moved to the fully advanced position. (The 10-to-30 m.p.h. acceleration figure in

the performance data was obtained with the ignition fully retarded at 10 m.p.h.)

Although 100-octane petrol was used, pinking was audible if the throttle was opened hard on full advance at any engine speed.

Moving the ignition lever to the one-third-retard position made it possible to thread dense traffic in a docile manner, but top was not engaged in 30 m.p.h.-limit areas. It was after the derestriction signs that the model really gathered itself up.

The close-ratio gears meant a drop of only 1,000 r.p.m. between first and second, 800 between second and third and 400 between third and top. As you might guess, acceleration was exceptionally rapid—guaranteed to satisfy the most hardened enthusiast.

The delightfully subdued drone from the siamesed exhaust system allowed full use of the performance without fear of causing offence. Because of the wide spread of power, upward gear changes were normally made at 5,400 r.p.m.— rather than at the ceiling of 6,800—equivalent to a corrected 50 m.p.h. in bottom, 66 in second and 80 in third. The speedometer read a constant 4 m.p.h. fast.

Tweaking the twistgrip half way continued the rush of the speedometer needle round to the 85 mark. The appallingly poor weather during the test period—continuous rain and mist—dictated cruising speeds no higher than 85 to 90 m.p.h.

A further tweak of the grip at ninety unleashed a fresh surge of power until the needle was hovering near the magic 100, but to achieve a genuine "ton" it was necessary to chin the tank top.

While not in the turbine-smooth category, the power unit was no rougher than one would expect of a vertical twin with high-kick pistons, and was commendably free of any noticeable vibration period.

COOL CLUTCH

In spite of being continually slipped in traffic, the clutch showed never the slightest sign of protest. Even after six full-throttle standing starts, when the performance figures were being obtained, only an insignificant amount of free play

Compression ratio of the engine is boosted to 9 to 1

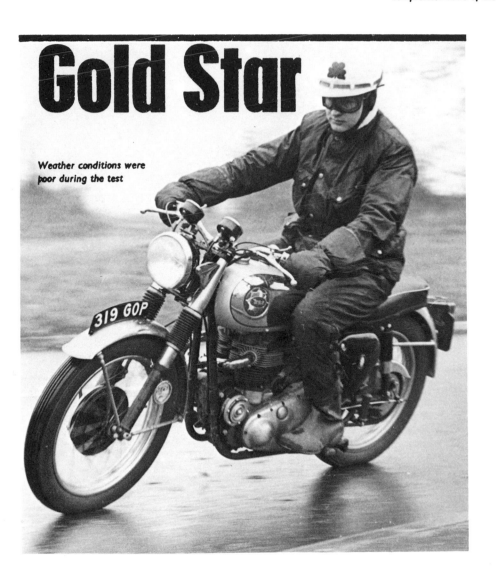

Gold Star

Weather conditions were poor during the test

319 GOP

appeared at the clutch lever; this free movement disappeared as the plates cooled.

The gear change was light and crisp in movement and positive at all times; neutral was easily selected from bottom or second.

After the front wheel had been balanced and both wheels correctly aligned, steering and handling were of true sporting class. Straight-ahead steering was precise up to 90 m.p.h. but then became progressively lighter until at maximum speed, 105 m.p.h. on a wet road, the front wheel tended to wander slightly. Tightening down the steering damper effected a partial cure.

NO BRAKE FADE

Roadholding and stability under normal conditions allowed high average speeds to be maintained safely. Stiffening the action of the front fork would probably eliminate a tendency for slight rolling on fast corners.

As befits such a high-performance model, both brakes were light in operation and extremely powerful. Initially, dust in the drum caused loud squealing from the front brake. In spite of repeated hard application from maximum speed, neither brake showed any tendency to fade, nor were they affected by prolonged riding in heavy rain.

The sharpened Super Rocket engine is housed in a Gold Star duplex-loop frame

The model was supplied with a down-turned touring handlebar. This brought too much weight to bear on the rider's wrists, particularly in traffic, so a more comfortable position was obtained by reversing the bar. A satisfactory compromise would be a shorter, straighter bar to provide slightly more forward lean without lowering the wrist level.

DE-LUXE SEATING

All controls were well placed for ease of operation and a reasonable range of adjustments is allowed. A more prominent dipswitch lever would have been preferred.

Well shaped and deeply upholstered, the dual-seat provided exceptional comfort no matter what mileage was being covered. It did not need a very long run in the rain, however, to prove the drawback of a narrow sports front mudguard

—the amount of road filth that blows back on the machine and rider.

Lighting was adequate for mile-a-minute cruising after dark and the dipped beam was satisfactory. Loud enough for jaunts about town, the horn would have to be more penetrating to be much use during fast, open-road touring.

Accessibility for routine maintenance tasks was good, but the tool kit did not include a spanner for adjusting the rear wheel. The roll-on centre stand required only moderate effort to operate, but its feet were too sharp; parking places had to be carefully chosen, for the legs would gradually dig into tarmac. A prop stand is available at extra cost.

The Rocket Gold Star, then, is that rare bird, a high-performance motorway express which is almost equally at home in less exciting urban surroundings.

PERFORMANCE DATA

(Obtained at the Motor Industry Research Association's proving ground at Lindley, Leicestershire.)

MEAN MAXIMUM SPEED: *Bottom 63 m.p.h.; *second 83 m.p.h.; *third 101 m.p.h.; top 103 m.p.h. *At 6,800 r.p.m., makers' recommendation.

HIGHEST ONE-WAY SPEED: 105 m.p.h. (conditions: slight tail wind, heavy rain; rider wearing two-piece suit and overboots).

MEAN ACCELERATION:

	10-30 m.p.h.	20-40 m.p.h.	30-50 m.p.h.
Bottom	5 sec	4 sec	3 sec
Second	—	5.8 sec	4.8 sec
Third	—	7.6 sec	6.2 sec
Top	—	8.4 sec	8 sec

Mean speed at end of quarter-mile from rest: 86 m.p.h.
Mean time to cover standing quarter-mile: 15 sec.

PETROL CONSUMPTION: At 40 m.p.h., 82 m.p.g.; at 50 m.p.h., 71 m.p.g.; at 60 m.p.h. 66 m.p.g.; at 70 m.p.h., 61 m.p.g.

BRAKING: From 30 m.p.h. to rest, 39ft (surface damp tarmac).

TURNING CIRCLE: 15ft 6in.

MINIMUM NON-SNATCH SPEED: 19 m.p.h. in top gear (ignition fully retarded).

WEIGHT PER C.C.: 0.64 lb.

SPECIFICATION

ENGINE: B.S.A. 646 c.c. (70 × 84mm) overhead-valve twin. Crankshaft supported in plain bearing on timing side and a ball bearing on drive side; plain big-end bearings. Light-alloy cylinder head; compression ratio 9 to 1. Dry-sump lubrication; oil-tank capacity 5¼ pints.

CARBURETTOR: Amal Monobloc; air slide operated by handlebar lever.

IGNITION and LIGHTING: Lucas magneto with manually operated advance and retard; Lucas dynamo charging 6-volt, 13 amp-hour battery through voltage-control regulator. Lucas 7in-diameter headlamp with prefocus light unit.

TRANSMISSION: B.S.A. four-speed gear box. Gear ratios bottom 8.39 to 1; second 6.34 to 1; third 5.25 to 1; top 4.78 to 1. Multi-plate clutch with bonded friction facings. Primary chain, ½ × 0.305in in light-alloy oil-bath case. Rear chain, ⅝ × ¼in with guard over top run. Engine r.p.m. at 30 m.p.h. in top gear, 1,850.

FUEL CAPACITY: 4 gallons.

TYRES: Dunlop: front, 3.25 × 19in ribbed; rear, 3.50 × 19in. K70 Gold Seal.

BRAKES: 8in-diameter front, 7in-diameter rear; finger adjusters.

SUSPENSION: B.S.A. telescopic front fork with hydraulic damping. Pivoted rear fork controlled by Girling three-position spring-and-hydraulic units.

WHEELBASE: 57½in unladen. Ground clearance, 6½in unladen. Seat height, 31in unladen.

WEIGHT: 415 lb fully equipped and with full oil tank and approximately half a gallon of petrol.

PRICE: £323 8s including British purchase tax.

ROAD TAX: £4 10s a year.

MAKERS: B.S.A. Motor Cycles, Ltd., Armoury Road, Birmingham 11.

DESCRIPTION: Motor Cycle, 8 February 1962.

Triumph Sports Cub

It stands to reason that if you want better quality, you have to pay more for it, and likeable though Triumph's little 199 cc Tiger Cub may have been in standard form, the Sports Cub version was a more expensive but far sturdier job. And so it should have been, sharing as it did many of the attributes of the competitions Cubs.

To recap on Meriden history, a Trials Tiger Cub had been catalogued in the late 1950s, but since it sported a standard-type front fork complete with nacelle-mounted headlamp, one could hardly accuse the makers of being serious about it.

But the Tiger Cub family began the 1960s with the benefit of an entirely new crankcase assembly, in which the timing-side casing incorporated the gearbox, while the drive side embodied the primary case. Based on this engine, new and tougher trials mounts were evolved by the factory competitions department for Triumph teamsters such as Ray Sayer, Gordon Blakeway, and Roy Peplow.

But not only was there a T20T Trials Cub in the 1961 programme; there was, too, a model listed as the T20S/L Scrambles Cub. Intended mainly for export to the USA, this was really the first Sports Cub. Discarding the fork-top nacelle, it featured a separate headlamp on brackets from the fork shrouds, while downstairs a sports camshaft and a 9 to 1 (instead of 7 to 1) compression ratio helped to boost the power output from the standard Tiger Cub's 10 bhp to a much more businesslike 14·5 bhp.

The official trials team popped up in the results at regular intervals (Johnny Giles won the West of England event in 1961, in addition to doing well in the Scottish Six Days Trial), but early in 1962 the news began to spread that Triumphs were going to build for sale a batch of genuine works-replica trials models, features of which would be a front fork with two-way hydraulic damping—in fact, the same fork as used on the 350 cc 3TA twin—plus a heavier-duty oil pump, and a more robust crankshaft with a larger-diameter big-end bearing, and a ball main bearing instead of a bush at the timing side.

Trials fans banged in their orders straight away, with the result that no fewer than *thirty* Triumph Cubs appeared in the entry for the 1962 Scottish Six Days Trial! Scott Ellis put up the Best 200 cc performance, while an Army trio, all on Trials Cubs, grabbed the Services Team Award.

This was fine, but the same press release that gave news of the works-replica trials model had given news, also, of a new super roadster, to be designated the T20S/H Sports Cub—the first mention of the model by this name. It carried the same strengthened crankshaft and ball main bearing as the trials mount, but continued the 9 to 1 compression ratio of the scrambler. Other details included rectifier-and-battery lighting, a quickly-detachable headlamp, and a larger fuel tank (3 gallons, instead of the 2⅜ gallons of the standard Tiger Cub).

From that point on, the Sports Cub was on its way, from year to year taking the benefit of improvements pioneered on the models used by the works trials and moto-cross riders.

Identification point for 1963 on all Cubs was the adoption of finned, cast-light-alloy rocker box covers instead of plain, and on the Sports Cub a rev-meter could be supplied if the customer so wished. Still the developments continued (for 1964, a solid crankpin and, for longer life, an oil-pump driving worm made from aluminium bronze). For all that, the oil pump appeared to be something of an Achilles heel of Cub design, and it would be a couple of years yet before the designers got things to their liking.

The 1965 season was a further landmark in the life of the Cubs and, especially, the Sports Cub. That year, the Scrambles Cub was dropped, and the home-market 199 cc range comprised the

Feet-up over the loose boulders of Laggan Locks in the 1962 Scottish Six Days Trial goes Scott Ellis, winner of the 200 cc Cup on his 199 cc Triumph Tiger Cub

Unexpected location for a Tiger Cub Engine was in Martin Legg's 1964 drag bike, known as 'Time Traveller'

Trials Cub, standard Tiger Cub, and Sports Cub, with the addition of the Mountain Cub for export to the USA only.

New throughout was a graphite-impregnated sintered bronze big-end bearing. A folding kick-start pedal appeared on the Trials and Sports models and, for the Sports Cub, came the heftiest front fork yet—from a Bonneville, no less!

Visitors to Meriden around this time may have been puzzled to see batches of Cubs painted drab olive green and equipped with pannier frames and similar military accoutrements. The reason was that the Cub had gone into service with the Danish and French Armies (although not with the British Army,

Inside view of the 1963 199 cc Triumph Sports Cub unit. By this time there was a duplex primary chain, and the contact breaker had moved to a location in the timing case. Power output was 14·5 bhp at 6,500 rpm

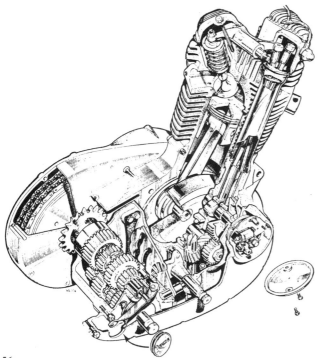

curiously enough). The Mountain Cub was a lot more colourful, painted in bright yellow and equipped with rifle clips.

In truth, the Mountain Cub was the first British-built trail bike, and was intended for the use of hunting enthusiasts in the USA. The bright yellow colouring was a safety precaution, a measure of protection against the trail-riding hunter from being shot at by other trigger-happy 'hunters'.

Through all of this, a little news item which appeared in February, 1965, could well have been overlooked. Because of the demand for Triumph twins, it said, the Cub production line was to be moved to the BSA premises at Small Heath, Birmingham. But there was more to it than that, because the BSA-Triumph group was moving towards greater integration of the two marques.

That became evident when the 1966 range was announced. At last the Cubs had a totally new oil pump—totally new for them, that is, because it was actually the slide-type pump that had been used on the vertical twins since 1937 or so. The Sports Cub and TR20 Trials Cub remained in the programme, but significantly there were two newcomers, the Tiger Cub and Super Cub, which discarded the familiar Meriden frame and, instead, made use of the frame, front fork, wheels and (on the Super Cub) fuel tank of the 175 cc two-stroke BSA Bantam.

The main differences between the standard Cub and the Super Cub were in the matter of trim, the former having a painted tank of the old Tiger Cub pattern, and the latter a chromium-plated BSA Bantam tank with Triumph badges.

The change was not necessarily for the bad, and a test of the Bantam-framed standard Cub showed that, if anything, the model felt a shade bigger than the genuine Meriden-bred article. A new Amal Monobloc 375/44 carburettor (without air slide) was specified, and this gave the machine a remarkable 96 mpg consumption figure at a steady 50 mph.

But, sad to say, BSA-Triumph were adopting a 'biggies only' policy, and 1967 brought the end of the line for both the Bantam and Cub. Uneconomical to build, said those in command, and the tooling for both models was promptly scrapped. It is too late now to argue the whys and wherefores, but in retrospect it does seem to have been a very mistaken policy. The absence of British lightweights from the shops meant that a youngster had to buy foreign for his first bike. And it was only natural that, when he wanted to advance to something bigger, he would return to the same dealer—and buy something bigger but of the same foreign make.

ROAD TESTS OF NEW MODELS

MERIDEN BABY WHICH CAN SHOW ITS HEELS TO MANY A BIG 'UN

199 c.c. Triumph Sports Cub

HEARD the lads talk of the Baby Bonnie? This is the model they mean; and just a brief run is enough to give a clue to the nickname, for crammed into a 199 c.c. pot is a helping of the same kind of boisterous energy which characterizes the 649 c.c. Bonneville twin.

Just look at the performance figures! Over 70 in top, and just 20s for the standing quarter. A showing like that would be no disgrace to a three-fifty. Certainly the Sports Cub is a little more pricey than the standard Tiger Cub roadster. But for the extra £22 the customer gets an engine which is virtually that of the scrambles model, 9 to 1 compression ratio and all, with the benefit of a beefed-up bottom-end assembly, more robust oil pump and increased oil supply.

In addition, the fork (which has two-way damping) has internals similar to those used on the Tiger 90 three-fifty; and there is a gear box with close third and top ratios, and a detachable headlamp with plug-in connection to the wiring harness.

Oddly enough, the first impression of the riding position is that the seat appears somewhat high. That's an optical illusion, for at 31in seat height both feet of an average-stature rider can be firmly planted on the roadway. It isn't that the rider is way up there: it is merely that the bike is way down here! And (again, oddly enough) the lean-forward attitude dictated by the low, flattish handlebar seems to emphasize the small size.

But there's nothing tiny about the Triumph's heart. A bit thumpy at low engine speeds, maybe, in that firing strokes could be felt as tremors through the footrests and handlebar. But open the grip and the power comes flooding in, sending the revs soaring up the scale and smoothing out the delivery.

This model is meant to buzz, and for it to produce its best the revs have to be kept up—which, of course, is where that close gap between top and third ratios pays dividends.

Change-up speeds? Say, 40 in second, 60 in third. Play tunes on the box, and the bike will sing along in the sixties with no bother at all.

Mark you, that 9 to 1 compression ratio makes itself felt when the time comes to kick-start. A really hefty jab at the pedal is called for—and two-hundred or not—an exhaust-valve lifter or compression-release valve would be a worth-while addition.

But it is all a matter of acquiring the knack. No carburettor air slide, but that doesn't matter much. A fairly liberal flooding of the carburettor, and the engine got cracking at about the third kick even on a frosty morning.

Down-for-down, up-for-up on any Triumph; and on the Sports Cub there was never any doubt about gear engagement. And it was easy enough to find neutral with just a flick of the toes.

However, before the first start of the day, it was found best to depress the starter pedal a time or two with the clutch withdrawn, just to free the plates.

Safety Plus

Heavy rain, black ice, half-gales; this test had the lot—and there was a heartfelt vote

Following pages: last of the Triumph 199 cc line, the Bantam Cub employed BSA frame and cycle parts (*Andrew Morland*)

SPECIFICATION

ENGINE: Triumph 199 c.c. (63 × 64mm) overhead-valve single. Steel-back, white-metal big-end bearing, crankshaft supported on two ball bearings. Light-alloy head; compression ratio, 9 to 1. Oil-tank capacity, 2¼ pints.

CARBURETTOR: Amal Monobloc with gauze-element air filter.

IGNITION and LIGHTING: Lucas RM18 alternator with coil-ignition, auto-advance and emergency-start circuit. Lucas 8 ampere-hour battery charged through silicon-crystal rectifier. Lucas detachable 6in-diameter headlamp with 30/24-watt main bulb.

TRANSMISSION: Triumph four-speed gear box in unit with engine. Gear ratios: bottom, 19.8 to 1; second, 13.4 to 1; third, 8.6 to 1; top, 7.13 to 1. Multi-plate wet clutch. Primary chain, ⅜in duplex, in oil-bath case; rear chain, ½ × 0.205in with guard over top run. Engine r.p.m. at 30 m.p.h., 2,850.

FUEL CAPACITY: 3 gallons.

TYRES: Dunlop, 3.00 x 19in ribbed front; 3.50 x 18in studded rear.

BRAKES: 5½in-diameter front and rear.

SUSPENSION: Telescopic front fork with hydraulic damping. Pivoted rear fork controlled by Girling suspension units.

WHEELBASE: 50in unladen. Ground clearance 8½in unladen. Seat height 30in unladen.

WEIGHT: 240 lb, with approximately one gallon of petrol.

WEIGHT PER C.C.: 1.2 lb.

PRICE: £188 8s, including British purchase tax.

ANNUAL ROAD TAX: £2 5s.

MAKERS: Triumph Engineering Co Ltd., Meriden Works, Allesley, Coventry.

PERFORMANCE DATA

MEAN MAXIMUM SPEED:
Bottom: *28 m.p.h. Second: *42 m.p.h. Third: *66 m.p.h. Top: 74 m.p.h. *Valve float occurring.

HIGHEST ONE-WAY SPEED: 77 m.p.h. (conditions: moderate rain showers, strong three-quarter wind, rider wearing two-piece suit and overboots).

MEAN ACCELERATION:

		10-30 m.p.h.	20-40 m.p.h.	30-50 m.p.h.
Second	... ...	4.6 sec	5.4 sec	—
Third	... ...	—	8.6 sec	8.6 sec
Top	... ...	—	11.0 sec	9.2 sec

Mean speed at end of quarter-mile from rest, 63.8 m.p.h. Mean time to cover standing quarter-mile, 20 sec.

PETROL CONSUMPTION: At 30 m.p.h., 118 m.p.g.; at 40 m.p.h., 100 m.p.g.; at 50 m.p.h., 86 m.p.g.; at 60 m.p.h., 72 m.p.g.

BRAKING: From 30 m.p.h. to rest, 32ft (surface, damp tarmac).

TURNING CIRCLE: 12ft 9in.

MINIMUM NON-SNATCH SPEED: 20 m.p.h. in top gear.

of thanks to the makers for the light, low-down weight and precise handling which eased the job of negotiating the dicey patches. Against that, the howling gusts which caught the model on passing side-street junctions could certainly be felt by the rider.

And there were one or two relatively fine days, when the Cub could be let off the leash. So full marks for the nicely tucked-in footrests, which meant that the little sportster could be heeled through a bend with no fear of anything grounding.

Suspension, particularly at the front, seemed a little too firm for orthodox tastes, but that's how sports-model fans like it; and a stiffish front fork certainly does improve navigation on a twisty section of road.

No trouble in making a getaway from a standing start on M.I.R.A.'s 1-in-4 test hill, with the clutch fully home before many feet had been covered. And here's a point: the Tiger Cub has never been noted for unobtrusiveness, but the mute fitted in the silencer tail pipe of the Sports Cub did a grand job of chopping the edge from the characteristic bark, even under hard acceleration.

Lighting was above expectations, permitting the use of relatively high cruising speeds at night, though the location of the dip-switch button on the top face of the headlamp shell was rather inconvenient.

Handsome? Hmm; let's say cobby, rather. The Sports Cub looks a goer, and in this case looks don't lie. It's a model which is enormous fun to ride—and watch out, you two-fifty merchants; this is a Cub with claws!

Triumph T120 Bonneville

A few readers may disagree with the choice, but if I had to pick out just one bike as *the* British motor cycle of the 1960s, I would plump unhesitatingly for the Triumph Bonneville—known affectionately by riders the world over as the 'Bonnie'. Introduced at the very last minute into the 1959 Meriden programme (it was not even listed in the early editions of the 1959 Triumph catalogue), it was still there in the 1981 equivalent, 22 years later; there have been, of course, many changes over the years. In 1959, it was a 650 cc pre-unit job with (for 1959 only) the famous Triumph nacelle headlamp. In the early 1980s, it was a unit-construction 750 cc machine with, at option, full electric starting and cast light-alloy wheels.

Between times, the Bonnie covered itself in glory in production-machine racing, all but died in the financial collapse of the BSA-Triumph group, was sentenced to death by the incoming NVT management, was absent from the market during the 18-months workers' sit-in, and came back to life under co-operative ownership.

Inevitably, it was pressure from the USA for more power that led Meriden to investigate ways of wringing still higher performance from the 649 cc Tiger 110 sports engine. But there was a limiting factor, because the crankshaft was still the old three-piece-suite (two half-shafts, bolted through flanges to a separate central flywheel) that had characterised Triumph twins—the 3T excepted—since Edward Turner's first 498 cc Speed Twin of 1937.

The design department came up with a one-piece shaft, over which a flywheel ring could be threaded, then secured to a central boss by radial studs. With this stronger crankshaft, the search for more power could continue. In the USA, Triumph-powered projectiles had been prominent since the mid-1950s in speed record attempts on the Bonneville Salt Flats of Utah, notably by Johnny Allen and Jess Thomas who each topped the flying mile at over 214 mph. The name of the new twin-carburettor sports twin, the T120 Bonneville, was a tribute to the salt-flats heroes.

The 1959 Bonneville had a deceptively sedate appearance, with fully-shrouded fork legs, touring handlebar, and the original type of single-down-tube frame. But the 1960 version was radically different. Not only was there a new duplex-tube frame and revised steering geometry, but the sporting image was

Rare version of the Triumph Bonneville was the Thruxton Bonnie production racer catalogued for 1965. With racing seat and fairing, it was a replica of the models raced by Percy Tait and Fred Swift

strengthened by the use of a quickly-detachable chrome-plated headlamp, gaitered fork legs, and twin Amal Monobloc carburettors fed from a single float chamber suspended by rod from a rubber diaphragm. An alternator was fitted for lighting purposes, but magneto ignition was retained.

Although around this time production-machine racing had not yet achieved the boom of later years, it was beginning to get a hold, with the Thruxton 500-mile marathon as the highlight of the season. In consequence, Triumph offered a list of racing goodies including a timing cover which incorporated a rev-meter-drive mounting, and a humpy racing seat.

The process was to culminate in the full-blown Thruxton Bonneville exhibited on the Triumph stand at the 1965 Blackpool Show. Complete with racing seat and fairing, and priced £30 above the roadster Bonnie, it was a replica of the model which (shared by Percy Tait and Fred Swift) had taken second place in the 1964 Thruxton 500-Mile race, and the reason for cataloguing it was that under the Thruxton regulations, no machine could qualify for entry unless at least 100 examples had been sold to the public through conventional channels.

Before then, though, the Bonneville had undergone a drastic redesign, to emerge for 1963 as a unit-construction model, fired by coil ignition and housed in yet another new frame, this time a reversion to single-down-tube style. The Bonneville's handling had not been everything it should be, but with the arrival of Doug Hele (a refugee from Norton) things improved. In particular, a more substantial tie-up between the frame loops and the ends of the rear fork pivot held frame whip effectively in check, while changes in the head angle gave precision steering.

In the USA, Gary Richards had clocked 149·51 mph on an unfaired Bonneville as early as' 1960, upping that figure to 159·54 mph the following year. British Triumph fans concentrated more on the production races which were gaining

The Bonneville adopted unit construction in October, 1962, at the same time mounting the contact-breaker on the end of the exhaust camshaft. New, too, was the trapped-ball method of operating the clutch thrust rod

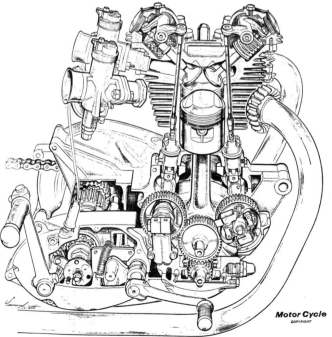

Motor Cycle
COPYRIGHT

Man on the 649 cc Triumph is none other than film star Dean Martin. He used the bike instead of a car to go to and from the studios daily

momentum, with the addition of the Hutchinson 100 to the long-established Thruxton event.

It was in 1967 that enthusiasm reached a peak, with the staging of the first Production-machine TT in the Isle of Man. Naturally, Bonnevilles dominated the 650 cc field, and to the 1967 Thruxton laurels (a win for Percy Tait and Rod Gould, with Joe Dunphy and Ray Pickrell as runners-up) could now be added the Proddy TT crown; winner John Hartle returned a commendable 97·1 mph average speed, and four more Bonnevilles—and a Tiger 110—finished in the first 11 places.

In the spring of 1969, Percy Tait brought more joy to Meriden by scoring his second Thruxton 500-Miles victory in three years, with other Bonnevilles filling second, fifth, sixth and seventh places. Better yet was to come, when Welshman Malcolm Uphill won the 1969 Production-machine TT at an average speed of 99·99 mph, having scored the first 100 mph-plus Island lap by a production machine from a standing start.

Nevertheless, 1969 was virtually the Bonneville's farewell year where production-machine racing was concerned, because by that time an even more potent model, the three-cylinder Trident, was poised ready to take over the torch.

The roadster Bonneville was still a public favourite, but the fates were poised to give it a heck of a wallop, from which it would take a long time to recover. BSA and Triumph had embarked upon a course of integration and, accordingly, had established an expensive 'think-tank' of boffins at Umberslade Hall, a country mansion beween Birmingham and Stratford-on-Avon.

One outcome was a new frame, based on a thin-wall backbone tube which would serve also as an oil reservoir, and this frame was intended to be used by both Small Heath and Meriden. However, it ran into many problems, and while these were being sorted out the Triumph production lines ground to a halt for more than three months.

When the frames did start coming through, it was found that the Bonneville engine would not fit—and the seat height was 2 in too elevated for the height of the average rider.

It did all get sorted out eventually, but what happened next is really a story of the 1970s and, thereby, beyond the scope of this particular book.

THINK of a superlative, double it . . . but no, don't even try. Words alone cannot amply describe the Bonneville 120, cold figures can but hint at the performance. It looks immensely powerful, sturdily and solidly built, yet set off by a glamour finish of white and lacquered gold. Given its head, it will whistle up into the treble figures, smoothly and safely. But there is also a fair helping of sweetness and humility down in the lower reaches of the rev band.

Built for the chap who travels far and fast, the Bonnie has a specification which borders on the brutal, embracing twin carburettors, 8.5 to 1 compression ratio and a power curve which climbs to 46 bhp at 6,500 rpm, then stays at that right up to the 7,000-rpm mark.

Such a model could be a real handful in city streets—lumpy, erratic, straining at the leash. But not so. How it's done is a Meriden mystery (though coil ignition and auto-advance come into it), for the Bonnie emerges as a gentlemanly, unobtrusive, tractable traffic-threader, quite amenable to being trickled along at 30 mph (or slower) in top, the grip only fractionally off the stop.

For all its urban docility, though, this is a Tarzan in city suiting—remarkably patient but with an underlying longing for freedom. Leave built-up areas behind, open the grip that little bit more and you'll note with surprise (though not alarm; the model is too well-bred to cause alarm) that the needle is much farther round the dial than you had imagined it to be.

That's mainly because the power flows in as a surging tide rather than as a noticeable kick in the pants.

Brisk even in the lower

649 CC TRIUMPH BONNEVILLE

Twin carburettors and an 8.5 to 1 compression ratio all help to give exciting performance. Note the lighting and ignition switches on the right

229KNX

Left is the revmeter, right the speedometer. The revmeter is an extra.

At that, there was no feeling of distress, either mechanical or personal.

In high-speed work, riding position is all-important. In this respect the Bonnie cannot be faulted. Maybe the seat is a little high for short-leg riders, but at least the model can be laid into a bend without anything grounding. The handlebar is nicely placed to allow a wind-cheating forward lean.

Long, sweeping curves find the big Triumph at its best, for on the latest unit-construction version there is rock-steady navigation all the way—no slow-speed roll, no over-the-ton weaving.

Suspension at front and rear is firm, yet extremely comfortable. The result is a machine which remains eminently controllable, whatever the circumstances.

No air slides are fitted to the carburettors, so for a cold-morning start there is need to flood both float chambers fully.

reaches, acceleration becomes shattering from 65 mph onward in top gear.

Use the gear box, changing from 48 mph in bottom, 66 mph in second and about 90 mph in third—and you find the sort of acceleration which, by rights, should be kept for the sprint strip.

That 14.6s figure for the standing quarter-mile was repeated time and again.

Cruising speed is difficult to pin-point. If time was not pressing there could be quiet pleasure in a 45 mph amble, the engine spinning over lazily, the exhaust note just a gentle, low-pitched drone. Yet if 65 or even 85 mph was your aim, the Bonnie would play along with amiable nonchalance.

Naturally enough, it is only

on a motorway that the machine can break out its true colours. Less congested, far more scenic than M1, the M5 road was chosen for a mid-week run.

Heading westward into a blustery wind, 100 mph was shown on the clock with the rider sitting up and feet on the normal rests. However, an electronic check showed that the speedometer was wildly optimistic, and the true speed was more like 90 mph. Still pretty good, though.

For the return run, the pillion rests were brought into use. Chin on the tank, it was possible to hold an indicated 120 mph for a full 15 miles. All highly flattering—but 7,000 said the revmeter, and that is equivalent to a true reading of 108 mph.

Battery, tool roll, tyre pump and oil-tank filler cap are located under the dual-seat which is hinged along the left side

The engine department produces a beefy 46 bhp at 6,500 to 7,000 rpm, but in traffic it is a thorough gentleman

SPECIFICATION

ENGINE: *Triumph 649 cc (71x82mm) overhead-valve twin. Plain big-end bearings; crankshaft supported in two ball bearings. Light-alloy cylinder head; compression ratio 8.5 to 1. Dry-sump lubrication; oil-tank capacity, 5 pints.*
CARBURETTORS: *Two Amal Monoblocs, 1 1/16-in-diameter chokes.*
IGNITION and LIGHTING: *Lucas RM19 alternator, charging six-volt, 12-amp-hour battery through rectifier; coil ignition with auto-advance. Quickly detachable (multi-pin and socket connection) 7in-diameter headlamp with 30/24-watt main bulb.*
TRANSMISSION: *Triumph four-speed gear box in unit with engine. Ratios: bottom, 11.81 to 1; second, 8.17 to 1; third, 5.76 to 1; top, 4.84 to 1. Primary drive by 3/8in duplex chain in oil-bath case; final drive by 5/8x3/8in chain with guard over top run. Engine rpm at 30 mph in top gear, 1,940.*
FUEL CAPACITY: *4 gallons.*
TYRES: *Dunlop or Avon (Avon on test machine): 3.25x18in ribbed front, 3.50x18in studded rear.*
BRAKES: *8in-diameter front, 7in-diameter rear with floating shoes.*
SUSPENSION: *Triumph hydraulically damped telescopic front fork. Pivoted rear fork controlled by Girling dampers adjustable for load.*
DIMENSIONS: *Wheelbase 55in unladen. Ground clearance 5in unladen. Seat height 31½in unladen.*
WEIGHT: *399 lb, including approximately 1½ gallons of fuel.*
PRICE: *£326 13s 3d, including British purchase tax. Revmeter £8 3s 8d extra. Pillion footrests £1 5s 1d, extra.*
ROAD TAX: *£4 10s a year; £1 13s for four months.*
MAKERS: *Triumph Engineering Co, Ltd, Allesley, Coventry.*

PERFORMANCE DATA

(Obtained at MIRA Proving Ground, Lindley, near Nuneaton.)
MEAN MAXIMUM SPEEDS: *Bottom, *53 mph; second, *70 mph; third, 96 mph; top, 110 mph. *Valve float occurring.*
HIGHEST ONE-WAY SPEED: *112 mph (conditions; damp track, light tail wind. Rider wearing one-piece leathers).*

MEAN ACCELERATION:

	10–30 mph	20–40 mph	30–50 mph
Bottom	2 sec	1.8 sec	2.4 sec
Second	3.2 sec	3 sec	2.6 sec
Third	—	4.4 sec	4.4 sec
Top	—	5.6 sec	5.4 sec

Mean speed at end of quarter-mile from rest: 94 mph.
Mean time to cover standing quarter-mile: 14.6 sec.
PETROL CONSUMPTION: *At 30 mph, 100 mpg; at 40 mph, 88 mpg; at 50 mph, 78 mpg; at 60 mph, 66 mpg; at 70 mph, 54 mpg.*
BRAKING: *From 30 mph to rest, 30ft 6in (surface, dry asphalt).*
TURNING CIRCLE: *15ft 10in.*
MINIMUM NON-SNATCH SPEED: *18 mph in top gear.*
WEIGHT PER CC: *0.61 lb.*

Then, too, the high compression ratio calls for a really beefy swing of the kick-starter pedal, but that is a knack which is easily acquired.

Excellent indeed is the lightness and gradual take-up of the clutch operation, provided by the new scissors-pattern thrust-rod mechanism. And there is unexpected lightness in the twistgrip movement; though the grip operates two throttle slides simultaneously, the effort required is no more than on a conventional single-carb model.

With the engine cold, gear engagement was entirely noiseless, though on this particular model it became somewhat clashy when working temperature was reached, unless care was taken to change up slowly and deliberately, and to accompany downward changes by a slight blip of the throttle.

VALVE GEAR

Again, a warm engine brought an increase in audibility of the valve gear, though no more than is acceptable for a super-sports machine.

Pleasantly subdued at moderate speeds, the exhaust note became flatter and more noticeable under hard acceleration, but it was not objectionable.

Good by normal standards, the electrics were a little disappointing in view of the Bonneville's high potential. Too, the placing of the lighting switch (on the left mid-riff panel, below the dual-seat nose) was decidedly inconvenient, making it difficult to change from pilot

to main beam when on the move, and precluding the giving of a warning flash from the headlamp when overtaking.

Just about adequate—but no more—for town work, the electric horn proved useless at higher speeds.

Not new, but a highly creditable feature for all that, is the pedal extension fitted to the Triumph centre stand. The Bonnie is admittedly bulky, yet it could be parked without the slightest effort.

A prop stand is also provided and this, too, was very simple to operate.

Braking is well in keeping with the general nature of the performance. The smooth and gentle retardation provided by the front brake, in particular, contributed greatly to the pleasure of using the machine in the manner for which it was intended.

After several hundred miles of heavy towsing there was no sign of oil leakage from the engine, but one silencer bolt had been lost, allowing some gas leakage at the joint between silencer and exhaust pipe on that side.

A few criticisms, then—but they pale into insignificance when set against the overall picture of a machine which must be not far short of the ultimate in super-sports luxury.

Made to be ridden hard, it *was* ridden hard; and the amount of enjoyment it provided is something which can never be listed in a mere performance summary.

The centre stand is very easy to operate—this is helped by a pedal extension on the left. Pillion footrests were fitted after pictures were taken

Following pages: Triumph's prestigious T120 Bonneville was in production throughout the 1960s. This is how it looked in 1960 (*National Motorcycle Museum*)

Norton ES400

In itself, the electric-start 384 cc Norton twin hardly qualifies as one of Britain's truly great motor cycles. But it did originate on the drawing board of one of our most illustrious designers— Bert Hopwood, no less, the man responsible for such all-time greats as the Norton Dominator, BSA Golden Flash, and Triumph Trident. Not only is it technically interesting, but it represents the small-capacity Norton vertical twins (the others were the 249 cc Jubilee and 349 cc Navigator), and on that score alone it merits attention.

Strictly speaking, the ES400—originally known as the Norton Electra—was not a Birmingham-bred model, but was brought into being at the AMC factory in Plumstead, after Bracebridge Street production had ended. Its life was a short one, spanning the period from January 1963 to the liquidation of AMC in mid-1966, but its origins went back to the 249 cc Jubilee which had been announced in November, 1958.

That model was indeed a Bracebridge Street project, and the 'Jubilee' name marked the 60 years since James Lansdowne Norton had founded the Norton Manufacturing Company in August, 1898, to produce cycle chains and fittings. All the same,

by 1958 Nortons were well and truly a part of the AMC empire, and a policy of integration demanded that the new lightweight should make as much use as possible of existing chassis parts. That is why the first Jubilees were virtually four-stroke Francis-Barnetts, using what was in essence the frame of the Francis-Barnett Light Cruiser with its part-tubular, part-pressed-steel construction. The front fork, front mudguard, headlamp and wheels were also Francis-Barnett items, while the extensive tail pressings, smaller versions of those featured on the Dominator 88 and 99 de Luxe, were produced by FB's presswork subsidiary, Clarendon Pressings.

However, the power unit was the really interesting part, and here Bert Hopwood had broken new ground in various directions. The crankshaft was a one-piece iron casting, with big-end journals the same size as those used on the Dominator

The ES400 was a descendant of the 250 cc Norton Jubilee, here seen in de Luxe form with the then-fashionable tail panelling and well valanced front mudguard. Frame members and other pressings were produced by Francis-Barnett—and it looked like it!

Actual capacity of the ES400 was 397 cc. Note the planetary reduction gearing at the end of the electric starter motor, and the sprag-type freewheel outboard of the crankshaft-mounted alternator. Electrics were 12-volt Wico-Pacy with relay-type automatic voltage control

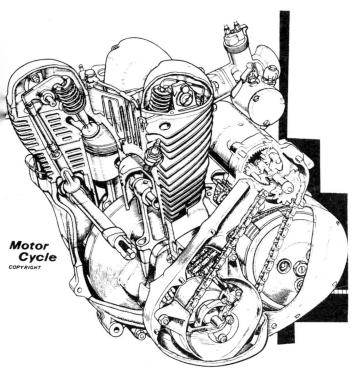

Motor Cycle
COPYRIGHT

twins. Cast-iron cylinder barrels were separate, and embedded for almost half their height in the crankcase mouth. Also separate, the light-alloy cylinder heads embraced a 'back to front' rocker arrangement, with the valves inboard of the pushrods; valve clearance was adjusted by means of eccentrically-mounted rocker spindles.

The Jubilee had genuine unit-construction of engine and gearbox, although the gear assembly (except for the clutch) was that of the semi-unit 248 cc AJS/Matchless lightweights.

Demonstrably a tourer, the Jubilee did not appear to have any competitions potential, but intrepid specials-builder Bob Collier thought otherwise. Over the years he had taken (and was to take) some very odd pieces of machinery through the Scottish Six Days Trial, and for the 1960 event he proposed to take a 249 cc Jubilee—in as standard a condition as may be—hitched to a Watsonian Bambini glassfibre scooter sidecar, into what turned out to be the final year in which a sidecar class was included in the Scottish.

Even with a 70-tooth rear sprocket fitted, the outfit had to be charged at the observed hills, with Bob and crewman Gordon Wilde giving as much leg assistance as they could. The weekly Press reported that the Jubilee's climb of the Ben Nevis sections, on the Wednesday run, was 'the fastest yet'. It had to be; it was the only way the little outfit could get to the top. Not only did Bob and Gordon finish the trial, but they gained a first-class award.

Late in the 1960 season a cheaper (and more handsome) 'standard' edition of the Jubilee was announced, with conventional mudguards in place of the voluminous pressings. And something else was on the boil, because within a few weeks a 349 cc twin had joined the range. This was the Navigator, very much on Jubilee lines but with a number of essential differences.

For one thing, the very oversquare Jubilee dimensions of 60 × 44 mm bore and stroke were replaced in the Navigator by 63 × 56 mm. That meant a new crankshaft, and in view of the extra power output it was decided that this should not be cast iron, but forged steel.

For the same reason, the two cylinder barrels were cast en bloc (although separate barrels were retained for the Jubilee). A Norton Roadholder front fork was substituted for the Francis-Barnett item, and Norton hubs with Dominator-size brake drums completed the specification.

But at the end of 1961 AMC shareholders were given the shock news that the group was diving into the red. Retrenchment was necessary, and that included closing Bracebridge Street and moving Norton production in with AJS and Matchless. Very few Norton personnel were willing to transfer to the alien south, and so when the Berliner Motor Corporation, AMC's USA distributors, made tentative enquiries about a bigger, electric-starting Navigator, the challenge was taken up by the Matchless drawing office.

The first two prototypes, sent to America late in 1962, were actually 397 cc models, achieved by boring the Navigator block out to its practical limit of 66 mm bore and, at the same time, lengthening the stroke to 58 mm. The latter change, however, proved to be unnecessary, and the production Norton Electra settled down at 384 cc (66 × 56 mm), retaining the Navigator crankshaft.

Electric starting was effected by mounting a Lucas M3 starter motor (as fitted to the 1981 Triumph Bonneville, incidentally) at the rear of the cylinder block. On the end of the starter motor was carried a sun-and-planet epicyclic mechanism affording an initial 5·4 to 1 reduction, and from there a chain drove to a sprocket incorporating a sprag mechanism, on the remote end of the engine shaft, outboard of the alternator. Overall reduction worked out at 11·14 to 1. A 12-volt electric system was necessary to operate the starter motor, and this included a 12-volt Wipac alternator and 12-volt, 12-amp-hour Exide battery.

Norton silver and black was the livery adopted for the ES400, but in the few years remaining the Jubilee and Navigator appeared with various colour schemes, including a deep translucent burgundy. However, AMC's financial worries were growing ever more desperate, and the abbreviated Norton range for 1966 as published by *Motor Cycle* embraced the Jubilee and ES400, but discarded the Navigator. Curiously, though, handlebar-tip direction indicators—possibly the first to be fitted as standard to a British motor cycle—were included in the ES400's British-market price of £259 10s.

In its short time of production, the ES400 did not really have time to get established. But its little kick-starter brother, the Jubilee, became the subject of a *Motor Cycle* reader's report published in August, 1965. In general, owners liked it, but there were a number of uncomplimentary remarks, especially in respect of oil leaks, poor dealer service and dodgy Wipac electrics. As one correspondent summed up: 'The Jubilee fills a vacant spot in the current range of British bikes, that of a 250 cc four-stroke twin, for which there is an obvious demand. But unfortunately, it doesn't fill it as well as it might.' Similar comments could probably have been made of the ES400.

Following pages: the 1964 ES400, which resulted from adding electric starting and raising capacity of the Norton Navigator unit (*National Motorcycle Museum*)

ROAD TESTS OF NEW MODELS

Mudguards are chrome plated. The starter motor nestles behind the cylinder block

384cc NORTON

APART from its extra 35 cc, three up-to-the-minute features distinguish the 384 cc Norton ES 400 twin from its famous sister, the Navigator. They are 12-volt electrics, push-button starting and grip-tip winkers. Other, less obvious, differences are that the steering head on the ES 400 is gusseted while the rear brake is of 7in diameter compared with the Navigator's 6in.

With the engine not too cold, the electric starter worked a treat. But it was hard put to spin the crankshaft fast enough for reliable starting when the ES 400 had just spent a frosty night in the open. The best drill then was to use the kick-starter initially—a couple of prods sufficed—and press the button for subsequent starts.

Incidentally, it is not necessary for the gears to be in neutral when using the electric starter. If a gear is engaged you merely declutch.

Along with the headlamp dip switch and horn button, the starter button is incorporated in a Wipac Tricon ring switch just inboard of the left hand-grip. On the other side of the bar, the winker switch could not be operated without releasing the twistgrip: an improvement would be to change this switch to the left.

Grip angle proved comfortable though reach to the clutch and front-brake levers was a shade on the long side. The footrests were low enough to give a wide knee angle but the starter-drive case fouled the rider's left leg.

Burbling unobtrusively through dense traffic or swinging along the open road at 70 mph came alike to the ES 400. Though healthy, the exhaust note was not objectionable; the twistgrip could be tweaked hard without giving offence.

Bottom-end punch was good without being startling—the engine gave its best results in the middle and upper rpm range. On the open road it was usual to let speed build up to an indicated 45 mph (true 42) in second and 60 mph (true 56) in third before changing up.

The needle would climb steadily to the 70 mark and anchor itself there on half throttle. Full throttle brought a further 5 mph and under favourable conditions, with the bulkily clad rider normally seated, the needle would hover on 80 indefinitely.

Provided the engine was allowed to spin freely, hill climbing was first class; only the steepest main-road gradients pulled the speed down appreciably.

Few vertical twins are vibrationless but the ES 400 is no great sinner. A tremor was felt through the handlebar when the engine was spinning fast but was never at any time uncomfortable.

Light and smooth in operation, the clutch showed no objection to a succession of six full-throttle standing starts when the performance figures were obtained. But, before the first start of the day it was advisable to free the plates by pumping the kick-starter with the lever pulled up to the handlebar.

Well chosen, the lower three gear ratios are slightly higher than on the Navigator, though top is the same.

Movement of the gear pedal was light and short. Noiseless upward changes were easily made but downward changes required precise blipping of the throttle if slight clashing of the dogs was to be avoided.

There was not the slightest difficulty in identifying the characteristically precise Norton steering. Absence of top hamper contributes to effortless handling and the ES 400 could be placed almost to a hair and cornered with utter confidence.

With the footrest rubbers well chamfered in the 2,000 miles already logged by the ES 400, the only limits to cornering angle were the centre-stand extension on the left and footrest hanger bolt on the right. Stability on slippery surfaces was remarkable.

Firm at low speeds, the front fork cushioned road shocks well at higher speeds. In contrast the rear-suspension units were soft in action and this gave rise to slight pitching and occasional weaving on fast bumpy bends.

SPECIFICATION

ENGINE: Norton 384 cc (66x56 mm) overhead-valve parallel twin. One-piece forged-steel crankshaft supported in ball bearing on timing side and roller bearing on drive side; shell-type plain big-end bearings. Separate light-alloy cylinder heads; compression ratio 7.9 to 1. Dry-sump lubrication; oil-tank capacity 5 pints.

CARBURETTOR: Amal Monobloc; air slide operated by handlebar lever.

ELECTRICAL EQUIPMENT: Coil ignition with twin contact breakers. Wipac 85-watt alternator, with rotor mounted on left-hand end of crankshaft, charging two Exide 6-volt 12-amp-hour batteries (in series) through rectifier. Separate Lucas electric starter driving crankshaft by chain. Wipac 7in-diameter headlamp with 50/40-watt pre-focus light unit.

TRANSMISSION: Norton four-speed foot-change gearbox in unit with crankcase. Gear ratios: Bottom, 15.4 to 1; second, 9.62 to 1; third, 6.98 to 1; top, 5.72 to 1. Multi-plate clutch with bonded friction facings running in oil. Primary chain, ⅜in duplex in cast-aluminium oil-bath case. Rear chain ½ x 0.305in with guard over top run. Engine rpm at 30 mph in top gear, 2,400.

FUEL CAPACITY: 3 gallons.

TYRES: Avon: front 3.00 x 19in Speedmaster Mk II; rear 3.25 x 18in Safety Mileage Mk II.

BRAKES: 8in diameter front, 7in diameter rear, both with finger adjusters.

SUSPENSION: Norton telescopic front fork with hydraulic damping. Pivoted rear fork controlled by Girling spring-and-hydraulic units with three-position adjustment for load.

WHEELBASE: 50½in. Ground clearance, 6in. Seat height, 30in. (All unladen.)

WEIGHT: 354 lb. fully equipped, with full oil tank and approximately one gallon of petrol.

PRICE: £259 10s including British purchase tax.

ROAD TAX: £4 10s. a year; £1 13s. for four months.

MAKERS: Norton Motors, Ltd, Plumstead Road, Woolwich, London, SE18.

DESCRIPTION: Motor Cycle, 31 January 1963.

PERFORMANCE DATA

MEAN MAXIMUM SPEED: Bottom, 36 mph.*; second, 58 mph*; third, 75 mph; top, 78 mph. *Valve float occuring.

HIGHEST ONE-WAY SPEED: 83 mph (conditions: light tail wind; 13-stone rider wearing two-piece waxed-cotton suit and overboots).

MEAN ACCELERATION:

	10–30 mph	20–40 mph	30–50 mph
Bottom	3.4 sec	—	—
Second	5 sec	5.4 sec	5 sec
Third	—	7 sec	7.2 sec
Top	—	9 sec	9 sec

Mean speed at end of quarter-mile from rest: 73 mph.

Mean time to cover standing quarter-mile: 17.8 sec.

PETROL CONSUMPTION: At 30 mph, 81 mpg; at 40 mph, 79 mpg; at 50 mph, 64 mpg; at 60 mph, 51 mpg.

BRAKING: From 30 mph to rest, 32ft (surface, dry tarmac).

TURNING CIRCLE: 15ft.

MINIMUM NON-SNATCH SPEED: 16 mph in top gear.

WEIGHT PER CC: 0.92 lb.

ES 400

The head-on view on the left emphasizes the slimness of the ES 400 and the excellent positioning of the flashing turn indicators on the ends of the handlebar

Below: The ES 400 shares with the three-fifty Navigator its enviable reputation for unsurpassed roadholding. Stability on wet roads was outstanding

Brakes on the model tested were below Norton standard—both lacked bite and the rear was particularly spongy. However, stopping power from high speed was considerably better than is suggested by the figure in the performance panel.

Headlight intensity was markedly good, the wide beam spread allowing daytime cruising speeds to be used in absolute safety after dark, but a sharper cut-off to the dipped beam would have been appreciated by oncoming drivers.

It was a change to ride a machine with a strident horn note; that of the Norton was loud enough even for high-speed motorway riding.

Most routine maintenance tasks were easily carried out—but not so valve adjustment. This entailed removing the petrol tank; and detaching the exhaust rocker covers was a bit of a fiddle because of the proximity of the steering-head gusset plates. The adjustment itself, by means of eccentric spindles, is straightforward.

Some difficulty was experienced in replacing the tool box lid because of its distortion; it is secured by a single slotted screw.

Throughout the 700 miles of the test the power unit remained completely oiltight and oil consumption was negligible. Since the petrol tap has no reserve position a careful check had to be kept on mileage.

With hard riding, the refuelling range was about 150 miles—on the short side for a machine of this type.

Smartly finished in black and matt silver, with chromium-plated mudguards, the ES 400, provides a lot of fun and is certain of an enthusiastic following among those who want a "three-fifty" with the plus of more power and luxury.

Above can be seen the cast aluminium case enclosing the chain drive from the Lucas electric starter to the left-hand end of the crankshaft

Right: A separate set of contact points serves each cylinder. Access for adjustment merely involves removal of a cover held by two screws

Below: Matching the oil tank on the other side, the left-hand pannier compartment houses the tool roll and quickly detachable batteries

"Ah see that MacGregor has started motor cycling . . ."

Royal Enfield Continental GT

When a young rider gets a bike, his first move is very often to strip it of this and that, and substitute whatever the current fashion in bolt-on goodies may be, so that the model looks as unlike the catalogue job as possible. Twenty-odd years later, a vintage nut may come along, to rescue the delapidated heap from the dusty corner of a garage, and spend untold wealth on seeking the very bits necessary to restore it to original showroom order.

Customising takes many forms, and back in the mid-1960s the lads of the village usually wanted to pretend they were racers; so the vogue was for clip-on handlebars, glassfibre fuel tanks, humpy-back seats, swept-back exhausts, rear-set footrests and reversed gear pedals. There was no real harm in that, of course, save that a novice rider is not the best engineer in the world, and the quality of some of the cheap fittings made by back-street workshops was dubious in the extreme. More than one accident was caused by the dodgy welding of cheap clip-on bars giving way at the time of stress.

So, reckoned Leo Davenport, the former TT winner who was in charge of Royal Enfield in its latter years, if a lad was going to customise his machine into a pseudo-racer anyway, why not offer him a bike on which the customising has already been carried out—professionally, and therefore more safely, at the works? Leo passed the word to Reg Thomas, in the Royal Enfield drawing office, and the result was the cheerful little Continental GT.

In essence it was just a dressed-up Crusader Sports, but most competently done, and really eye-catching with a bright red tank (glassfibre had not yet been outlawed) carrying flamboyant Royal Enfield lettering in white, twin 'brake cooling' discs on the front wheel, chromium-plated exposed rear damper springs, and all the other trimmings to gladden the heart of an apprentice coffee-bar cowboy.

The beauty was more than skin-deep, too, because compression ratio had been raised to 9·5 to 1, the inlet port in the head was opened out and a 1⅛-in choke Amal Monobloc carburettor fitted—incidentally, with a bell-mouth intake instead of an air filter; but real racers didn't use air filters, anyway. Moreover, crankcase breathing had been entirely revised, the waste gases now making their way to atmosphere by way of a big-bore plastic pipe draped along the underside of the seat on the left-hand side and so to the tail of the rear mudguard; that, too, was the way the real racers did it.

In truth, the better crankcase breathing was long overdue, because the Crusader family of engines had for years suffered from high blood pressure. There is no denying that they went like stink, but the crankcase joints were anything but oiltight, nor did it help matters that many riders tended to overfill the gearbox. So take note, any reader thinking of restoring a little Enfield, that there is indeed a gearbox oil-level plug. It's the middle screw of the right-hand engine cover.

The Redditch people had certainly extracted good mileage from their 248 cc unit-construction power plant, which was first announced (as the Crusader) late in 1956 (work on it had begun in 1954). The inspiration had come from managing director Major Frank Smith, but the design work was the

The sheer cheek of it! Australia's Gordon Keith takes his 250 cc Royal Enfield Continental round the outside of Alastair Copland (650 cc Triumph Bonnevile) at Castle Combe. The machine was fourth in its class

department of Reg Thomas, and it was the first engine for which he had been given full responsibility. The company did not award Reg the title of 'designer', and his official status was Chief Draughtsman, with Chief Engineer Tony Wilson-Jones taking over the development of the engine to production form.

Very unusually for a small four-stroke single, the Crusader unit disposed its camshaft and pushrods on the *left*, in the same casing as the primary drive. Unusually, too, the Lucas alternator was on the right of the engine, in its own compartment where it would not become contaminated with primary-drive oil and sludge. More novelty was in the use of a one-piece cast-iron crankshaft, RR56 light-alloy connecting rod, and steel shell big-end bearing. Bore and stroke dimensions were well oversquare at 70×64.5 mm, and a generous overlapping of the main and crankpin journals provided a stiff and sturdy shaft assembly.

From the original Crusader, the family of unit two-fifties seemed to spread out in all directions, to encompass the Crusader Airflow (with voluminous dolphin-type touring fairing), a trials version campaigned with considerable success by Johnny Brittain, the Super-5 which introduced a five-speed gear cluster and a good but unpopular trailing-link front fork, the Crusader Sports, the Olympic Sports and, especially for the great Australian outback, a sheep-herding variant listed as the Wallaby.

The Crusader Sports had come on the scene in October, 1958, bringing a sportier camshaft with quicker-lift cams and more overlap. The public liked it on the whole, and one contributor to a *Motor Cycle* readers' survey declared it to be 'The most underrated bike on the market'. They liked the traditional rear hub cush-drive. They gave the brakes a resounding 90 per cent mark of approval. They declared it to be easy to work on, simple and reliable. But they also criticised the valve gear as noisy, slated the engine oil-tightness, and noted a lack of precision in the gear change, sometimes resulting in a box full of neutrals.

From experience, the imprecise gear change was especially noticeable on the Super-5, but to give credit to the Royal Enfield people, they did work at it, and the five-speed cluster of the Continental GT was a considerable improvement.

Uncharacteristically, and way outside their country-cousin image, the Royal Enfield people introduced the Continental GT in November, 1964, with real flair and showmanship and, of course, it paid off handsomely in the amount of publicity gained. The plot was that a model should be ridden from John O'Groats

As part of the publicity concerning the Continental's debut, John Cooper hammers the model around Silverstone for eight laps, averaging over 70 mph

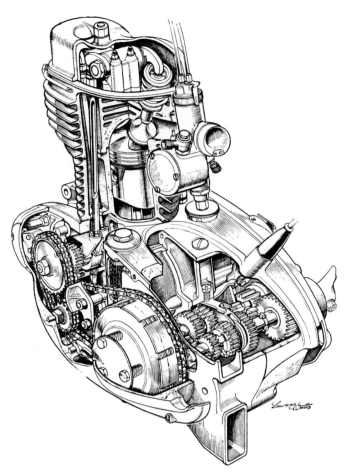

Basic power unit of the Crusader family, the clean, compact, 248 cc ohv four-speeder. One unusual feature is the timing sprockets on the same side as the primary chain. Note the duplex camshaft chain with slipper tensioner. The unit-construction power house has a common oil supply for engine and gearbox

to Land's End, with riders from the major motor cycle journals each taking a stint (*Motor Cycle* took over for the final stretch, David Dixon riding the Taunton to Land's End leg). The trip was completed in 24 hours but—and this was the imaginative bit—at Oulton Park and at Silverstone, well-known road racers took over for a quick blast. At Oulton, Geoff Duke ripped off five rapid laps, while at Silverstone, John Cooper took it round for eight laps (he lapped at over 70 mph, by the way).

It was perhaps a cafe-racer model. But it could give a good account of itself, for all that, and one or two found their way into club racing. A couple of the more enterprising Royal Enfield dealers (Gander and Grey, and Deeprose Brothers) went so far as to produce even sportier versions, and the Gander and Grey Gannet with its worked-on engine (10 to 1 compression ratio, bigger inlet port, lead-bronze big-end shells, race fairing and light-alloy wheel rims) was quite a serious racing tool.

There was no change in Continental GT specification for 1967—except for the USA, where they wanted a braced moto-cross handlebar to be fitted, heaven knows why—but that was its final year. On the stocks was a new unit-construction 175 cc overhead-camshaft model but, unfortunately, the monetary value of the Enfield Cycle Company Ltd was less than the site value of the Redditch works. Financiers moved in, closed down operations (although the Interceptor continued for a short while longer, built at Bradford-on-Avon by Enfield Precision Ltd) and sold the Redditch plant as an industrial estate. Asset-stripping, it's called.

248 cc ROYAL ENFIELD Continental GT

ROAD TESTS OF NEW MODELS

Above: The swept-back exhaust pipe accentuates the sporty lines of the neat power unit. Top: Handling is well up to par and the engine will push the model along at nearly 80 mph

"JOINED the coffee-bar crowd, then?" The questioner was Jeff Smith, leaning from his scrambles pick-up as the little red bike came alongside in heavy traffic. One couldn't help but grin. Clip-ons and rear-set footrests are not everyone's cup of Maxwell House.

Still, give a chap a hot two-fifty and it's a certainty that he will want to drape it about with bolted-on goodies. So (reasoned Royal Enfields), let's fit the doodahs and whatsits —revmeter and all—from the word go. Besides, a bike properly sports-tailored at the factory can be a better proposition than one to which clip-ons have been added by unskilled hands.

What emerges is just about the snazziest-looking sportster ever. There's a sleek, glass-fibre tank in fire-engine red, adorned by the Royal Enfield name in bold, white lettering; a huge breather pipe, in clear plastic, led to the tail of the machine; two big dummy brake-cooling discs on the front hub; a racing-style dualseat with a fashionable humped rear pad.

Real pay-off, though, is that the Continental GT goes every bit as well as it looks.

Anyway, not to worry about the riding position, which is more comfortable than it looks once you get used to it. This bike was never intended as a town runabout and inching forward in slow-moving traffic at rush hours does induce wrist-ache—

Following pages: made for the young-in-heart, the 1966 Continental GT was a best-seller of the Royal Enfield range (*National Motorcycle Museum*)

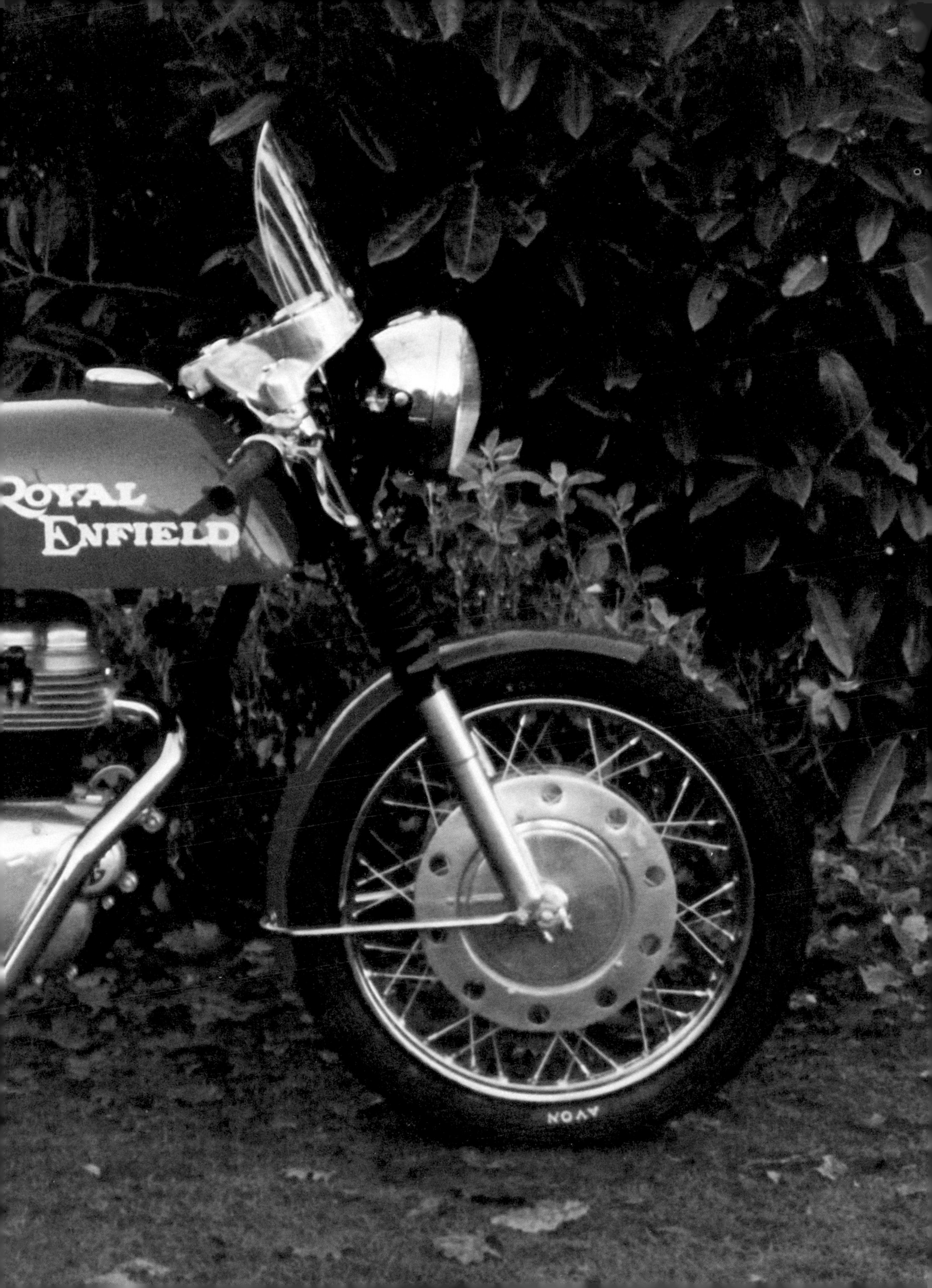
ROYAL
ENFIELD
AVON

but show it an open road, let it get into its stride, and it becomes a different bike altogether.

The low bars allow you to tuck your elbows in neatly; get down to it properly and watch the needle go soaring round the dial—past the 90 mph mark in favourable circumstances (this was on MIRA's outer circuit, be it added).

To produce the very best in performance, you keep an eye on the revmeter rather than the speedometer and change up at the peak bhp point (7,500 rpm) in each cog.

As on the majority of

is all one hundred per cent motor cycle, a complete machine rather than a collection of bits and pieces in a frame.

Nothing flaps, vibrates or rattles, while the celebrated vane-type shock absorber in the rear hub plays its part in keeping the power supply smooth all the way.

Nothing rattles? Well, maybe the valve gear does (clearances are bigger than is usual on a roadster) but even that is a solidly soothing sort of rattle, somehow quite appropriate.

example of friendly persuasion.

With both brakes used together, a stopping distance of 28ft 6in from 30 mph was recorded, a performance far above average. Nor did heavy braking at the end of a series of flat-out runs produce any sign of fade.

For an out-and-out sports model, the GT proved to be remarkably economical, returning a consumption figure of 115 mpg at a steady 30 mph. Understandably enough, the tank level sinks a bit more rapidly when the grip is held open, but not so rapidly as all that.

Nobody is going to grumble at 64 to the gallon at a maintained 70-per.

One of the most noticeable features of the Continental GT is the big-bore breather pipe. All very sporty-looking, but it isn't just for show.

On this model the designer has completely revised the breathing arrangements of the basic Crusader design, with the aim of overcoming past criticisms of external oiliness.

In that he has succeeded entirely. Through miles of hard riding the engine unit remained completely oil-free.

It *is* possible to ride a GT quite quietly through built-up

The sleek little Royal Enfield in its red-and-chromium-plate overcoat

machines, the speedometer was inclined to flatter; it read about 6 mph fast in the higher reaches.

Much of the credit for the high-average potential should go to the springing—a little on the soft side, but with impeccable damping which allowed the machine to float over the ripples as though it were a hovercraft.

Maybe it is sticking one's neck out to describe the navigation as faultless, but any doubters should try a GT for themselves.

Except for having somewhere to hang the twistgrip and control levers, a handlebar of any kind is well-nigh superfluous, for this is a machine which flows through the bends without a waver.

Most satisfying of all is the conviction you feel that this

Brake and gear-change pedals marry in nicely with the rear-mounted footrests and can be operated from the crouch without any awkward wiggling of the ankles.

Gear-pedal travel is extremely short and the cogs mesh cleanly, without clash or any effort.

Neutral is a shade tricky to find, particularly with the model at a standstill. It helps to permit the clutch just to bite while the pedal is eased upward from the second-gear position.

Both handlebar levers are long, ball-ended and light in operation.

Royal Enfield machines have a reputation for good braking, but the front stopper of the GT is surely the best that Redditch has yet produced. Not vicious, rather a prime

Paired speedometer and revmeter in the fork-top panel, together with the lighting switch

areas, by judicious use of the throttle, but when the throttle is used joyously the exhaust is apt to be raucous. Therein lies the only black against the model.

Lighting is well up to the mark, with a main beam amply bright for main-road cruising in the sixties at night. However, the ammeter can't be seen unless you sit up and peer over the flyscreen.

This is undoubtedly the finest two-fifty Royal Enfields have ever made, one which can be enjoyed every mile of the way.

It is sweet-natured and accommodating—built to go and built to stop. The factory are entitled to be proud of it.

Left : Impressive-looking front wheel with its bolted-on light-alloy discs and brake air scoop.   Right : Electrical equipment under the seat enclosed by a neat, glass-fibre shield

BOTTOM   **SECOND**   **THIRD**

FOURTH   **TOP**

Bottom-, second-, third-, and fourth-gear figures represent maximum-power revs, 7,500

THIRD

ROYAL ENFIELD Continental GT

ACCELERATION

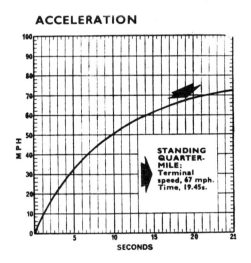

STANDING QUARTER-MILE: Terminal speed, 67 mph. Time, 19.45s.

MOTOR CYCLE Road Test

ENGINE
Capacity and Type: 248 cc (70 × 64.5mm) ohv single.
Bearings: Ball and roller mains; plain big-end.
Lubrication: Wet sump; capacity 3 pints.
Compression Ratio: 9.5 to 1.
Carburettor: Amal Monobloc, 1⅛in-diameter choke. Air slide operated by handlebar lever.
Claimed Output: 21 bhp at 7,500 rpm.

TRANSMISSION
Primary: ⅜ × 0.225in chain in oilbath case.
Secondary: ½ × 0.305in chain.
Clutch: Multi-plate running in oil.
Gear Ratios: 17.4, 12.82, 9.57, 7.52 and 6.02 to 1.
Engine rpm at 30 mph in top gear: 2,600.

ELECTRICAL EQUIPMENT
Ignition: Battery and coil.
Charging: Lucas 60-watt alternator to six-volt, 13-amp-hour battery through rectifier.
Headlamp: 6in-diameter with 30/24-watt main bulb.

FUEL CAPACITY: 3½ gallons.

TYRES: Dunlop Gold Seal: 3.00 × 18in ribbed front: 3.25 × 17in studded rear.

BRAKES: 7in diameter front; 6in diameter rear.
SUSPENSION: Telescopic front fork with two-way hydraulic damping; pivoted rear fork with Girling spring-damper units.
DIMENSIONS: Wheelbase, 52in; ground clearance, 5½in; seat height, 29½in. All unladen.
WEIGHT: 306 lb including half a gallon of petrol.
PRICE: £275 including British purchase tax.
ROAD TAX: £4 a year.
MAKERS: Enfield Cycle Co, Ltd, Hewell Road, Redditch, Worcs.

PERFORMANCE

(Obtained at the Motor Industry Research Association's proving ground, Lindley, Leicestershire.)
HIGHEST ONE-WAY SPEED: 85 mph (10½-stone rider wearing two-piece suit and boots; strong following wind).
BRAKING: From 30 mph to rest on dry tarmac, 28ft 6in.
TURNING CIRCLE: 18ft 6in.
MINIMUM NON-SNATCH SPEED: 17 mph in top gear.
WEIGHT PER CC: 1.23 lb.

FUEL CONSUMPTION

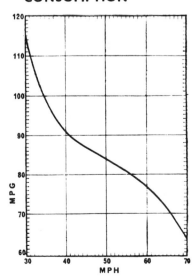

AJS Sapphire Ninety

Just why the design staff (or maybe the directive came from Higher Up) at the Woolwich plant of Associated Motor Cycles should have been so ornery, must remain one of life's little mysteries; but it was indeed so. For example, the very trim and pretty little two-fifty introduced in March, 1958, as the Model 14 AJS—or, if you didn't like the colour or the tank badge, the Model G2 Matchless—looked for all the world as though it were a unit-construction job in the modern idiom.

By that time, of course, virtually every new bike incorporated unit construction of engine and gearbox, for sound technological reasons. Indeed, AMC themselves used it in their new range of single-cylinder two-strokes. Yet here was their new four-stroke, still with the old-fashioned construction of separate engine and gearbox. This was not because this was a convenient short cut to make use of an existing gearbox design, either. This was the first quarter-litre model to emerge from Woolwich since pre-war times, so the box was quite new. The method of construction was cunningly disguised by extending the right-hand engine cover rearward, and by making the gearbox circular and locating it in circular openings in the rear engine plates. It was held secure by two metal straps.

Novel thought, maybe? Not a bit of it, because it was simply a reversion to the identical arrangement used on Model J and Model H Matchless twins as long ago as 1918!

Certainly there were some advantages, as designer Phil Walker explained. Primary chain adjustment was simply a matter of slackening off the gearbox clamp straps and rotating the entire box as necessary, thus doing away with the need to incorporate some form of jockey pulley or chain tensioner in the primary drive. Also, it made engine or gearbox overhaul or replacement much simpler.

In other respects, quite a lot of ingenuity had gone into the design, notably in the angled cylinder head (a light-alloy casting) adopted to give incoming gas a swirl effect. In typical Matchless style, hairpin valve springs were employed right up to almost the final season of production. A neat touch was the incorporation of a small (2½ pt) cast-light-alloy oil tank within the fore part of the right-hand engine cover.

At 69·85 × 64·85 mm bore and stroke, the engine was oversquare, and to minimise side thrust or piston slap the crankshaft was offset from the cylinder centre line by ¼ in (the désaxé effect). Compression ratio was 7·8 to 1, and an Amal carburettor with $1\frac{1}{16}$-in choke (unusually big for a two-fifty) was employed. The piston was wire-wound in its lower groove.

Frame design was relatively straightforward except that the

The AJS Sapphire 90 was not the first Woolwich product to use a cylindrical gearbox. The same principle was employed on this 1918 Model J Matchless twin!

engine cradle was a steel pressing, and the front fork was a lightweight telescopic component, similar to that of a James.

At first, only a roadster was available, but by September, 1958, a scrambler had joined the range. This was the AJS 14CS, and because it did have a bearing on the later two-fifties, it is worth looking at in detail. Chassis changes included a heavier-gauge frame front down tube, and the familiar Teledraulic front fork from the three-fifties. Internally there were lightened flywheels, a 10·5 to 1 compression ratio, and gear pinions made from 'a superior grade of steel' (which did not say much for the standard components!)

For 1961, the scrambler was further improved by the adoption of a new crankshaft assembly with larger crankpin and a heavier-duty connecting rod. Crankcase breathing was now by a direct vent instead of through a hollow bolt, and carburettor size had been upped to 1⅛-in choke. That season, too, the AMC models were all given names, and under AJS badges there were the 14 Sapphire, 14CS Scorpion Scrambler and (a newcomer) 14S Sapphire Sports. The Matchless equivalents were named G2 Monitor, G2CS Messenger, and G2CS Monitor Sports.

First mention of a still sportier two-fifty came in May 1962. This was the 14CSR Sapphire Super Sports, graced with the Teledraulic front fork and engine internals of the Scrambler, plus a larger inlet valve and lengthened induction tract. The wheels had full-width hubs, and the engine appeared to be all-alloy, but in fact the cast-iron cylinder barrel had a coat of aluminium enamel.

By this time the range of two-fifties was at its peak, with the choice of four models under each marque name, but now the tide was on the ebb. For 1963 the 14S Sapphire Sports, and 14CS Scorpion Scrambler were discontinued. In Britain, one never saw a Matchless or AJS 248 cc scrambler anyway, although it may have been different in the USA.

On to 1964, and out went the standard model, leaving only the 14CSR Sapphire Super Sports (and its Matchless buddy) to carry the flag. But in June of that year the machine was given a great boost when Peter Williams and Tony Wood, co-riders of a 14CSR prepared and entered by Tom Arter, pulled off a resounding victory in the 250 cc class of the important Thruxton 500-Miles.

Tony Woods heads his Sapphire 90 into a corner during the 1964 Thruxton 500-Miles. He shared the bike with Peter Williams and they won the 250 cc class at an average speed of 61·6 mph

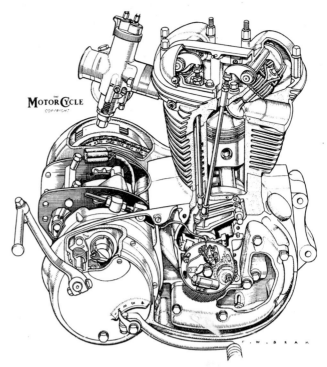

Unusual feature of the AJS/Matchless 250 cc engine was angled positioning of the cylinder head which, in turn, meant an unorthodox pushrod layout. The cylindrical gearbox was rotated to adjust the primary chain

During the early stages the little Ajay had held a consistent third spot behind the more flamboyant Honda and Montesa of the initial leaders. But after 3½ hours the pacemakers were out, and the steadily circulating AJS was into the lead. And there it stayed to the very end, winning at an average speed of 61·6 mph.

The last major changes in the design were made for the 1965 season, when the traditional hairpin valve springs gave way to coil, a new high-crown piston gave 9·5 to 1 compression ratio, and there was a closer-ratio gear cluster. For some unaccountable reason, too, the machine underwent another name change. The Model 14CSR bit remained (most youngsters translated the initials as 'Coffee Shop Racer', by the way—and handled the machine accordingly) but now it was the Sapphire Ninety; although if the 'ninety' was supposed to indicate its performance potential, it was very wide of the mark.

It was to survive for just one more season, 1966, when the machine was still catalogued by the financially-ailing AMC group amid a welter of Norton-engined Matchless and Matchless-engined Nortons. Final modifications were a swept-back exhaust pipe in the BSA Gold Star style, and light-alloy instead of chromium-plated mudguards.

So died what was a happy little machine that, on the whole, was well-liked by the younger set. Usually, it could be counted on for a top whack of 80 to 85 mph (although, to give of its best, good use had to be made of the gear pedal). Usually, too, it would cover 78 or so miles to the gallon if handled enthusiastically, or up to 100 mph if the rider was more prudent.

Certainly it had its faults, but these were mainly minor. The centre stand was too weak and sometimes allowed a bike to fall over when parked. A fractured gear selector spring was a regular occurence. Electrics (by Wipac) were not the most reliable that ever were. Spares from the factory and retailers were not always readily obtainable. And the small (2½ pt) oil tank capacity made it essential to carry out relatively frequent oil changes.

But it was a very forgiving little bike, for all that, and a particularly comfortable one to ride.

ROAD TESTS OF NEW MODELS
248 cc AJS SAPHIRE NINETY

LAST SUMMER saw this sports model really hit the limelight with a clear-cut class win in the Thruxton 500-Mile Race. Its success, which remained a talking point long after the meeting, was a reminder that the quarter-litre market is not the exclusive preserve of non-British manufacturers. Following this, in the autumn when the AJS 1965 range was announced, there was news of modifications to give more go to the Sapphire Ninety, as this 248 cc model is now named.

Coil valve springs replace the hairpin variety. Compression ratio is stepped up from 8 to 1 to 9.5 to 1 and gear ratios are closer than before. A larger-capacity silencer is fitted. It is tucked in and raised slightly to keep it out of the way when cornering.

First impressions mean a lot. When you straddle the Sapphire Ninety you are assured that AJS don't regard riders of two-fifties as necessarily on the small side.

Dimensions of the handlebar-seat-footrest set-up are such that whether your pals call you Lofty or Titch you should feel at home.

The handlebar is almost flat with slightly downswept grips and induces a forward lean rather than a crick-in-the-neck crouch. The riding position allows you to tuck in and adopt a relaxed, comfortable stance when hustling.

A criticism of the Matchless equivalent model tested in 1962 was that, on full lock,

Smooth contours give the power unit an attractive appearance and make cleaning easy

---

Specification and Performance Data

ENGINE: AMC 248 cc (70 × 65mm) overhead-valve single-cylinder. Double-row roller big-end bearing; crankshaft supported in a ball and a roller bearing on the drive side and a plain bearing on the timing side. Light-alloy cylinder head, cast-iron cylinder barrel. Compression ratio 9.5 to 1. Dry-sump lubrication; oil capacity, 2½ pints.

CARBURETTOR: Amal Monobloc 1⅛in choke; air slide operated by handlebar lever.

ELECTRICAL EQUIPMENT: Coil ignition. Wipac 54-watt, alternating-current generator mounted on drive-side crankshaft charging Exide 11-amp-hour battery through rectifier. Wipac 6in-diameter headlamp with pre-focus light unit and 30 24-watt main bulb.

TRANSMISSION: AMC four-speed gear box clamped to rear of engine. Gear ratios: bottom, 17.97; second, 11.68; third, 8.05; top, 6.51 to 1. Multi-plate clutch with bonded friction facings. Primary chain ⅜in duplex in cast-aluminium case. Rear chain ½ × 0.305in

with metal guide over top run. Engine rpm at 30 mph in top gear, 2,800.

FUEL CAPACITY: 3½ gallons.

TYRES: Dunlop: front 3.25 × 17in ribbed; rear, 3.25 17in studded.

BRAKES: 6in-diameter, front and rear; finger adjusters.

SUSPENSION: AMC telescopic front fork with hydraulic damping. Pivoted rear fork controlled by Girling three-position, spring-and-hydraulic units

DIMENSIONS: Wheelbase, 53in. Ground clearance, 5½in. Seat height, 30in. All unladen.

WEIGHT: 330 lb, fully equipped, including approximately one gallon of fuel.

PRICE: £224 18s 5d, including British purchase tax.

ROAD TAX: £2 5s a year.

MAKERS: Matchless Motor Cycles, Ltd, Plumstead Road, London, SE18.

DESCRIPTION: "Motor Cycle," 22 October 1964.

MEAN MAXIMUM SPEEDS: Bottom*, 31 mph; second*, 48 mph; third*, 70 mph; top, 82 mph. *Valve float occurring.

HIGHEST ONE-WAY SPEED: 83 mph (conditions: still air, rider wearing two-piece suit).

MEAN ACCELERATION:

	10-30mph	20-40 mph	30-50 mph
Bottom	3.8 sec	—	—
Second	4.6 sec	4.8 sec	—
Third	—	7.8 sec	6.8 sec
Top	—	11.2 sec	9.8 sec

Mean speed at end of quarter-mile from rest: 70 mph.

Mean time to cover standing quarter-mile: 19.4 sec.

PETROL CONSUMPTION: At 30 mph, 112 mpg; at 40 mph, 84 mpg; at 50 mph, 66 mpg; at 60 mph, 58 mpg.

BRAKING: From 30 mph to rest, 30ft (surface, dry tarmac).

TURNING CIRCLE: 14ft.

MINIMUM NON-SNATCH SPEED: 19 mph in top gear.

WEIGHT PER CC: 1.32 lb.

In any case, one soon became accustomed to the heaviness and then it passed unnoticed.

Suspension at both ends was firm and well damped and contributed to predictable handling when flicking the machine quickly through a right-left-right series of bends.

Rippled surfaces on metalled roads or pot holes on unmade tracks failed to catch the suspension off guard.

The power bonus makes itself felt in the middle and upper part of the range. There is an overall impression of increased liveliness, and the unit is remarkably free from vibration.

Bull point is that the added power has not been obtained at the expense of tractability.

The Sapphire would woofle along at 30 mph in top gear on a trace of throttle and without any fuss. At this pace in built-up areas there was just a subdued burble from the exhaust.

Mechanical noise was at a commendably low level, but the exhaust note became obtrusive at wide throttle openings.

The Smiths speedometer is easily read and was no more than 2 mph optimistic throughout the range. There is no trip mileage recorder, but the total mileage is shown to the nearest tenth.

For high-speed, open-road cruising, suitable gear-change speeds were 28, 40 and 60

one's thumbs could be trapped against the petrol tank. This does not occur on the Sapphire Ninety.

Almost smooth, plastic handlebar grips are fitted. They do not provide enough friction, especially when they are wet.

Control layout is good. Levers and pedals are correctly positioned for easy use.

During the test the AJS was ridden in a variety of weather conditions and over a variety of surfaces, some of them exceedingly slippery.

No praise is too high for the handling; the rider felt confident of staying in control at all times.

A trace of heaviness could be detected in the steering when traffic threading at walking pace, but this was more than offset by rock-steady adhesion to line at the other end of the scale.

Top: Handling is exemplary and inspires confidence at all times. Note the new silencer. Above: The Sapphire Ninety contrives to look up-to-date without recourse to unnecessary gimmicks

Following pages: no concours d'elegance winner, Mark Tudor's 1965 Sapphire 90 is a workaday machine which has given its owner long and faithful service (*Bob Currie*)

mph. The 1965, closer spacing of the ratios enhances the appeal of the machine. Happy cruising speed was 60 to 65 mph.

Restarting from a standstill on a 1 in 6 hill was accomplished without difficulty. The clutch could be fully engaged after covering the first yard or so.

Using third gear, main-road gradients were dismissed with nonchalance. This ratio (8·05 to 1) provided brisk acceleration for overtaking whether solo or two-up.

ZIPPY

In fact, acceleration in general, producing as it does a standing-start quarter-mile in under 20 seconds, is decidedly brisk and is more than adequate to hoist the model into the zippy class.

Gear selection is so smooth and easy that it immediately calls to mind the knife-through-butter cliché, although

Removal of the left side cover gives access to the ignition coil and rectifier. The battery is located under the seat

Excellent controllable braking is provided by the British Hub front brake. It maintained its performance during heavy rain

a shade less pedal travel would be preferred.

Ratios should be swapped as fast as the pedal could be operated.

The clutch engaged smoothly in normal usage, but full-power take offs when the standing-start quarter-mile figure was being obtained produced some snatching. There were never any signs of clutch drag. No adjustment was required throughout the period of the test.

Starting proved simple. It was advisable to leave the carburettor tickler alone and use the handlebar-mounted air-slide lever. The engine was sensitive to the air setting until the proper operating temperature had been reached.

NO PINKING

Fuel consumption was light, especially in view of the performance available. The engine performed quite happily on premium-grade petrol and showed no tendency to pink under heavy load.

Oil is contained in a separate sump on the right of the crankcase. Consumption was negligible even during sustained hard riding. Oil tightness was marred by a slight weep from the gear-box end cover.

Performance and handling can be exploited to the full only if matched by the brak-

ing. In this respect the AJS earned full marks. Both brakes were light in operation and efficient at all speeds.

Ventilation scoops are provided on the front brake but, on the test model, the slots had not been properly cleared of metal. However, no fading was experienced.

Lighting was adequate for 60-mph cruising after dark. The dipswitch has a wipe action; this is excellent as it ensures that there is no possibility of lag during the change from main to dipped beam or vice-versa.

Action of the lighting and ignition switches was spongy. A firm action with a positive click when the movement is complete would be more acceptable.

Accessibility for routine maintenance of rocker settings, contact-breaker, battery and other items is good. The tool kit supplied with the machine is adequate.

Thanks to the smooth contours of the power unit and liberal use of chromium-plating cleaning is a straightforward task.

The Sapphire's attractive finish is given the final touch by its blue and chrome and gold-lined petrol tank. Here is a bike which is easy on the eye; easy on the pocket for tax, insurance and fuel; and with its peppy performance, easy to have fun on.

Two screws secure the contact breaker cover on the right of the power unit. Points adjustment is easy

DMW Sports Twin

In the matter of motor cycle design ingenuity, the big battallions certainly had no monopoly on talent, and at least two of Britain's smaller manufacturers could produce machines packed with features that were truly brilliant. One such was Greeves, famous for its pioneer work with cast-light-alloy frame members and rubber-in-torsion front suspension. Another was DMW—and perhaps 'was' is the wrong term to use, because the company still exists, and although motor cycle production is currently rather low key, sophisticated telescopic front forks are currently marketed under the alternative Metal Profiles trade mark. Twice running, in the late 1970s, a 250 cc DMW with an engine of the firm's own make won the ACU Midland Centre trials championship.

By one line of descent, ancestry of the DMW can be traced back to the Wolverhampton-built Diamond of vintage years, touching HRD and taking in Calthorpe along the way, but the initials were originally those of Dawson's Motors, Wolverhampton, and the DMW name first appeared on the tank of some grass-track specials raced by W. L. ('Smokey') Dawson in 1938-9. Smokey was interested in suspension systems, too, and from 1940 onwards DMW—then in a very small way of business—began converting customers' bikes to swinging-arm rear suspension. They were among the first British makers to offer a telescopic fork (the DMW Telematic of 1944), and a full-width front hub with dual drum brakes, in 1945.

Production of complete motor cycles, powered by a 125 cc Villiers engine unit, began in 1947, and in those early years the make gained a high reputation in the competitions field, especially in the International Six Days Trial. But it was for the excellence of their roadsters that they were to become still better known, and the credit for this must go to pre-war BSA trials ace, Mike Riley, the company's designer and engineer.

Particularly noteworthy was the use made of square-section frame tubing (which permitted easy adaption to engines of various sizes and capacities) allied in some instances to pressed-steel and fabricated frame centre sections. The rear fork was a masterpiece, embodying snail-cam adjustment of the whole assembly just astern of the pivot point; the rear wheel spindle was a simple pull-out affair, and there was no way that the quickly-detachable rear wheel could get out of alignment.

Hubs and brakes were DMW's own, and they incorporated adjustment at the brake shoe fulcrum end, and a method of shoe expansion adapted from a Girling patent. A totally-enclosed rear transmission was an unexpected luxury on a Villiers-powered two-stroke. Some models even featured an automatic rear stop light, actuated on braking by a blob of mercury trapped in a tube, which surged forward under deceleration to make an electrical contact.

DMW were into road racing, too, initially with an overhead-camshaft 125 cc model known as the Hornet (although they supplied frames also for several of the home-built machines—DMW-Anelay, DMW-Enfield, etc—contesting the first post-war 125 cc TT races). The original Hornet employed a French AMC power unit, but with the arrival of the Villiers Starmaker the Hornet name was revived. Managing director Harold Nock assembled two Starmaker engines side-by-side, driving through a patented coupling system to a separate gearbox, but regrettably the twin (known as the DMW Typhoon) failed to live up to its early promise.

Most unusual DMW design of all was the 249 cc Deemster of the 1960s. In appearance it was a scooter, with small wheels and typically 'scooter' features such as legshields, footboards, and rear enclosure panels. Yet a closer look would reveal the twin-cylinder Villiers Mk. 2T engine housed in a normal 'motor cycle' position in the frame. Even more telling was the use of a conventional between-the-knees fuel tank.

In fact the Deemster was an all-weather, small-wheeled motor cycle, and though very few were sold to the general public, it was adopted in quite large numbers by the police of the West Midlands and rural Wales for beat patrol work. It was

The DMW was a bike with a sporting heritage. In this shot John Morris, of Bromsgrove, takes a 197 cc DMW single through a mountain village in the 1951 International Six Days Trial in Italy

Following pages: the DMW Sports Twin was an outstanding machine of its type. Shown is a 1962 model, at that time named the Dolomite II (*National Motorcycle Museum*)

A totally different type of 249 cc Villiers-twin-powered DMW was the Deemster—part scooter, part motor cycle. It was used by police in the West Midlands and Mid-Wales for rural patrol duties

particularly suitable for this kind of work, because the use of a small rear wheel allowed ample carrying capacity in the pressed-steel bodywork rear of the single seat for a first-aid kit, leggings, fluorescent jacket, rolled-up 'Accident' warning banner, clipboard, and other constabulary necessities. It had a radio handset on the tank top, too.

First appearance of the 249 cc Villiers 2T engine unit had been in 1956, and DMW (who are just along the road from the Villiers works) were first to incorporate the new engine in an extremely handsome roadster finished in maroon and brown. The model was really a development of the existing 224 cc DMW Cortina single, and was accordingly given the name Dolomite—Cortina being the name of an Italian resort in the Dolomite Mountains where Harold Nock had spent a winter holiday. (DMW had thought of Cortina as a model name long before Ford stole it, while at this stage British Leyland's Triumph Dolomite car was still some years off!)

In the years that followed, the DMW Dolomite twin was a permanent fixture in the company's programme. To choice it could be fitted with MP-Earles pivoted front fork instead of the telescopic type, and with electric starting on the Siba Dynastart system.

Around the middle of 1963, Villiers were faced with the problem of adapting their 249 cc twin for installation under the

A courageous DMW race design which did not live up to early promise was the 500 cc two-stroke-twin Typhoon, using Villiers Starmaker cylinders and gearbox on DMW's own crankcase assembly

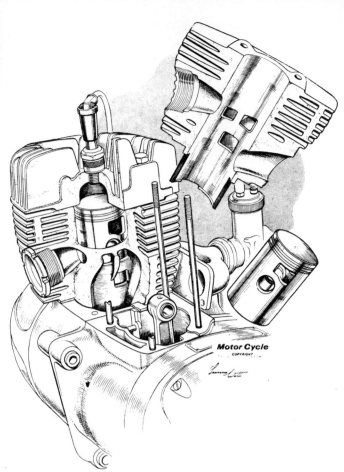

To provide increased air space between the cylinders, the Villiers Mk. 4T twin had shallower, but more numerous, transfer ports than the original Mk. 2T engine

bonnet of the Bond three-wheeler, and to allow for a greater passage of cooling air between the cylinders and over the heads the upper works were redesigned, with shallower transfer ports, and more of them, ported pistons, and angled head finning. The modified engine was named the Mark 4T.

For Bond installation, power output remained at 14·5 bhp, as with the Mk. 2T twin. However, the 1964 programme found the Mk. 4T superseding the Mk. 2T for motor cycle use also. By this time, power had been boosted to 17 bhp at 6,000 rpm, mainly through the fitting of an exhaust system with tuned resonances.

Not that the Mk. 4T was all sweetness and light, for it had a 'top-endiness' more characteristic of Japanese buzz-boxes than of the more sedate Mk. 2T, a point brought out in the road test which follows. Gone was the Mk. 2T's torquey bottom-of-the-rev-scale punchiness, and this was a particularly sad loss in so far as DMW's police Deemster was concerned. The Mk. 4T did not suit this 'plod around the parish' model at all, and after experimenting with a Deemster powered by a 197 cc Villiers Mk. 9E single, DMW redesigned the machine around the flat-twin two-stroke 250 cc Velocette Viceroy scooter running gear. It was not very successful.

But the Mk. 4T-powered DMW Sports Twin (successor to the Dolomite) was a totally different animal. It you can find one second-hand, grab it quick because the bike was a minor classic in its own little way. True, it tended to be ignored by the general public, and in consequence not many were built before Villiers ended proprietary engine production. But that was the public's loss.

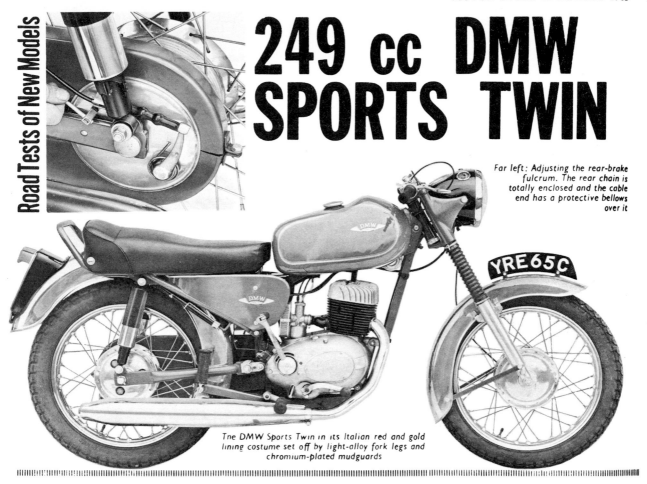

Road Tests of New Models

249 cc DMW SPORTS TWIN

Far left: Adjusting the rear-brake fulcrum. The rear chain is totally enclosed and the cable end has a protective bellows over it

YRE 65 C

The DMW Sports Twin in its Italian red and gold lining costume set off by light-alloy fork legs and chromium-plated mudguards

PARADE this little red beauty before a crowd of typical young riders and, following the Oohs and Ahs of admiration, someone will surely ask: " What's a DMW, then? " Not surprising, that, for the make is relatively uncommon outside its native west midlands. Certainly the DMW is British; it hails, in fact, from Dudley—where it has been built for 20 years or so. The engine is the familiar Villiers (in this instance, the Mark 4T twin) but it is the ingenuity of the cycle parts and the host of individual touches which sets the Dee-Em apart from the general run.

Thus the specification embraces polished, cast-light-alloy wheel hubs (the rear wheel quickly detachable) in which are remarkably powerful, tappet-action DMW-Girling brakes. Rear dampers are three-position Girlings and you don't often see those on a lightweight. Adjustment of the totally enclosed rear chain is achieved by moving the entire fork rearward, so ensuring that the wheel cannot get out of line.

Detail work extends to little plastic bellows protecting what would normally be the exposed ends of the brake cables and to aircraft-type locknuts on the engine, damper and mudguard-mountings.

It all adds up to a top-quality machine, a shade more expensive than the rest but worthy of the closest examination.

With a label such as Sports Twin, a sporty riding position is only to be expected. Nevertheless, it is not taken to extremes. What you get here is a short, flat handlebar, and seat and footrests an inch or so more rearward than on a touring job.

The result is a lean-forward, cheat-the-wind position which can be maintained for hours without strain on your wrists or back muscles. The welded-on handlebar lever pivots are rather more inboard than usual, though the levers themselves remain within easy reach and are pleasantly light in operation.

As a matter of personal preference, the dipswitch and horn button could have been nearer the left grip, but that's something an owner can decide for himself.

One further comment about the controls. The gear pedal could be reached readily with the tester's size nines, but folk with smaller feet might prefer a pedal fractionally shorter than the one supplied.

Surprisingly, this particular Mark 4T engine required only the merest tickle of the float chamber plunger when starting, with the air lever left severely alone and the twistgrip about one-eighth open.

This might seem to point to an over-rich mixture, yet the engine two-stroked quite happily and richness was certainly not reflected in the fuel-consumption figures.

This Villiers twin is a thorough-going smoothie, utterly devoid of vibration anywhere in its make-up and able to pour out power like cream from a jug.

Not that there is too much urge downstairs, for in the lower reaches of the rev band you have to sit tight and wait for the kettle to boil.

Still, the model is a sportster and demands to be treated as such. That means winding it up in each cog before selecting the next. If such a scheme is adopted, the DMW responds brilliantly.

In top gear, for example, the bike can plod along smoothly and sedately at around 25 to 30 mph, but the acceleration from that level is all but non-existent. For a real getaway,

Left: Bob Currie gives the model an airing in the country. Below: Adjusting one of the three-way rear dampers. Note the qd rear wheel

SPECIFICATION AND PERFORMANCE

ENGINE: Villiers 249 cc (50 x 63.5mm) two-stroke twin. Cast-iron cylinder barrels, light-alloy heads. Crankshaft supported in one ball and two roller bearings; roller big-end bearings. Compression ratio, 8.75 to 1. Petroil lubrication, ratio 20 to 1.

CARBURETTOR: Villiers S25 with mesh-type air filter. Air slide controlled by handlebar lever.

ELECTRICAL EQUIPMENT: Villiers six-volt flywheel generator with remote ignition coils. Exide type 3EV11, 12-amp-hour battery. Lucas 7in-diameter headlamp with 30/24-watt main bulb; type 8H horn; stop lamp.

TRANSMISSION: Villiers four-speed gear box in unit with engine. Gear ratios: bottom, 19.3; second, 12; third, 8.3; top, 6.3 to 1. Multi-plate clutch running in oil. Primary chain ⅜ x 0.225in in oil-bath case; rear chain ½ x 0.305in, totally enclosed. Engine rpm at 30 mph in top gear, 2,600.

FUEL CAPACITY: 3¼ gallons; reserve-type fuel tap.

TYRES: Dunlop K70. 3.00 x 18in front, 3.25 x 18in rear. Quickly detachable rear wheel.

BRAKES: 6in-diameter DMW-Girling front and rear.

SUSPENSION: Metal Profiles telescopic front and pivoted rear forks. Girling spring-and-hydraulic rear suspension units, adjustable for load.

DIMENSIONS: Wheelbase, 52in. Ground clearance, 5¼in. Seat height, 30in. All unladen.

WEIGHT: 307 lb with approximately half a gallon of fuel.

PRICE: £222 15s, including British purchase tax.

ROAD TAX: £4 a year.

MAKERS: DMW Motor Cycles (Wolverhampton), Ltd, Valley Road, Sedgley, Dudley, Worcs.

MEAN MAXIMUM SPEEDS: Bottom, 31 mph; second, 43 mph; third, 56 mph; top, 69 mph.

HIGHEST ONE-WAY SPEED: 69 mph (conditions: negligible side wind; 14½-stone rider wearing two-piece suit and overboots).

MEAN ACCELERATION:

	10-30 mph	20-40 mph	30-50 mph
Bottom	4s	—	—
Second	6.4s	5.2s	—
Third	—	8.4s	8.2s
Top	—	21.4s	13.4s

Mean speed at end of quarter-mile from rest, 60 mph.
Mean time to cover standing quarter-mile, 20 8s.

PETROIL CONSUMPTION: At 30 mph, 102 mpg; at 40 mph, 94 mpg; at 50 mph, 78 mpg; at 60 mph, 55 mpg.

BRAKING: From 30 mph to rest, 28ft 6in (surface, dry asphalt).

TURNING CIRCLE: 12ft.

MINIMUM NON-SNATCH SPEED: 18 mph in top gear.

WEIGHT PER CC: 1.23 lb.

it is necessary to drop down a couple of notches and take it from there; with 40 showing in third, snick into top and the model gets going like the favourite out of Trap One.

Any speed from 40 to an indicated 60-plus will serve as a comfortable cruising speed, with plenty more to come if needed. On two or three occasions, indeed, the 75 came up in favourable circumstances but that was not the strict truth, for an electronic check proved the dial to be reading around 5 mph high at its upper end.

Incidentally, the big-dial speedometer has a trip recording drum, another unexpected feature.

On gradients, speed does tend to drop away; it is necessary to slip into third fairly early so that a high average can be held.

Exhaust silence is well above average. The twin Villiers silencers so mute the note that it is almost entirely inaudible from the saddle at normal traffic speeds. Even when the machine is accelerated hard,

there is little more than a low-pitched drone.

Steering is noticeably light at low speeds, but once the Sports Twin hits its stride the handling is everything that could be expected from a factory with road-race experience.

For one-up riding, the rear dampers were set in the middle position, giving a firmish ride in keeping with the model's aim.

Ground clearance is excellent and the DMW can be heeled over extremely smartly

without any part scraping the deck.

A stopping distance of 28ft 6in from 30 mph tells only part of the story, for the brakes, though extremely effective, are far from harsh in operation. In particular, lightly stroking the front-brake lever brings an immediate check to forward progress, firm yet gentle.

On the electrics side, the Sports Twin scored further high marks. A night-time run showed that the 7in-diameter

headlamp offers near-daytime cruising potential with a beam both broad and bright; the dip-switch provided a good action.

One last surprise was that here, for once, was a two-stroke with a loud and effective electric horn.

Smartly finished in Italian red, with gold-lined fuel tank, polished light-alloy fork legs and chromium-plated mud-guards, the DMW Sports Twin is a machine to which the makers, obviously, have given a great deal of thought.

BSA Bantam D14/4

'Who's to say that there won't be a Bantam with us another 20 years from now?'—I wrote that concluding sentence of the 1968 Bantam road test which follows. The answer, alas, was not all that long in coming, for although few people realised it at the time, the BSA Group's financial problems were such that the poor little Bantam was to have its neck wrung late in 1971; it was, said BSA, no longer economic to produce. There *should* have been an updated Bantam, and the back-room staff at Umberslade Hall (the BSA Group's country-hideaway think tank) produced drawings showing a very smart little job with square-edged crankcase castings not unlike those of a Sachs. Sadly, there was no longer the money available to finance the necessary tooling-up.

The earlier history of the Bantam was chronicled in *Great British Motor Cycles of the Fifties*, but to briefly recall this, the model started life in 1948 as a mirror-image replica of the pre-war DKW RT125, plans of which had been passed to BSA as war reparations. From the original rigid-frame 125 cc Bantam, a steady progress through the 150 cc Bantam Major had led to the 173 cc (61·5 × 58 mm bore and stroke) D7 Bantam Super as introduced for the 1960 programme; details included an unusual lubrication system whereby oil from the gearbox looked after the crankshaft main bearing on the ignition side, while a bleed from the primary chaincase oiled the drive-side main.

In plunger-sprung form, the basic 125 cc D1 was continued (mainly for Post Office use) right through to 1963, selling at under £120 all-in. Most of the development was concentrated on the 173 cc version, which gained a Torrington needle-roller (instead of plain bush) little-end bearing for 1961, while in the same year a chromium-plated fuel tank and plastic name badges became available at around £4 extra.

However, the first really significant change came in July, 1966, when the D7 models (standard, and de luxe) were replaced by the new D10, featuring a 40 per cent increase in power output. Achieved by modified porting, discs attached to the flywheels to increase primary compression, a domed instead of flat-top piston, oval connecting-rod shank, and an increase in compression ratio from 7·4 to 8·65:1, the D10 now produced 10 bhp at 6,000 rpm and, on test, reached 64 mph yet without sacrificing bottom-end punch.

But that wasn't all, because by the end of the year there were no fewer than *four* D10 models, comprising the bargain-basement three-speed D10 Silver Bantam, four-speed D10 Bantam Supreme, D10S Bantam Sports, and D10B Bushman.

The Sports justified its name by featuring a humpy-backed

The D14/4 Bantam could have been a best-selling trials model, if only BSA had given proper backing to their own competitions department. Dave Rowland—here climbing Grey Mare's Ridge—finished second to the illustrious Sammy Miller (Bultaco) in the 1967 Scottish Six Days Trial, and two other Bantams won Special First Class awards

'racing' seat, handlebar flyscreen, chromium-plated mudguards and headlamp, full-width wheel hubs, a high-level exhaust system—and, believe it or not, a strip of stick-on chequered plastic tape down the centre of the tank top.

And the Bushman? That one was a workhorse, primarily for sheep-herding on Australian farms or for riding the mountain trails of the USA. Coloured a distinctive tangerine and white so that it could be spotted from afar, the Bushman used 19-in diameter wheels, and featured a high-level exhaust and sump protector plate.

The Bushman obviously had the makings of a useful little trials bike, and BSA competitions manager Brian Martin now proceeded to investigate its possibilities by building himself a Bushman with C15-type front fork, Victor Enduro air cleaner, and other bits and pieces selected from bikes in the existing Triumph and BSA ranges.

Brian collected first-class awards in the 1966 Colmore and St. David's national trials and, encouraged by this success, Mick Bowers built a similar model for his own use. Even more adventurously, Brian Martin entered a works team for the Scottish Six Days Trial, comprising Dave Rowland (riding Brian's experimental bike), Bowers (on his own privately-built model), and Dave Langston (on a special 148 cc machine constructed in the competitions department at Small Heath).

The results far exceeded the hopes of the little knot of dedicated Bantam fans working at BSA, virtually in defiance of management policy. Dave Rowland finished runner-up, and both Langston and Bowers collected special first-class awards.

This was the time when BSA should have exploited such a success by marketing a small batch of trials Bantams. No special parts were required, and even though such competition models would have to be specially built, rather than left to the tender mercies of the production-line assemblers, the extra cost would have been more than outweighed by the advertising benefits of seeing the BSA name once more in the results lists, week after week.

But by this time the men at the top were well out of touch. The market for trials machines, as they saw it, was too small to bother about.

The D10 Bantams were to remain in production for little more than a single season, being replaced by the new D14/4 series from September, 1967. Power output had been raised still more and now stood at 13 bhp at 5,750 rpm, the gain resulting from fatter flywheel pads (so increasing primary compression still more), wider transfer and deeper inlet ports, and a redesigned head. Also, the exhaust pipe diameter had gone up substantially, from $1\frac{1}{4}$ to $1\frac{5}{8}$ in and there was a long, tapering exhaust.

Even this was not the final flowering of the Bantam, because there was yet another revamp early in 1969, with a diecast cylinder head, revised crankshaft, and modified crankcase castings. The Sports and Silver Bantam versions had been discarded, and now there were just the standard D175 Bantam, and D175B Bushman. Yet for all the improvements, the Bantam was under sentence of death, the last batch being built in late 1971 and offered, at bargain prices, by Cope's of Birmingham at the 1972 Midland Motor Cycle Show.

There were still those who believed passionately in the Bantam, and they included Brian and Michael Martin, and Mick Bowers. Desperately, they pleaded with the BSA management to be allowed to form a consortium, to take over the Bantam tooling and continue on a smaller scale within the group. 'There was still a potentially lucrative Post Office contract to be gained,' explains Mick Bowers, 'and the trials market would have been sufficient to keep a small unit employed. But nobody wanted to know.'

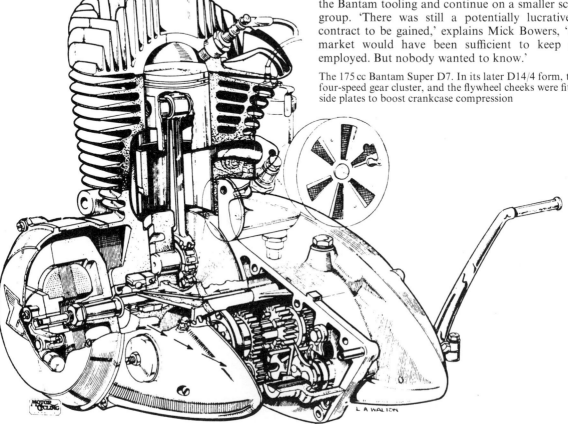

The 175 cc Bantam Super D7. In its later D14/4 form, the unit had a four-speed gear cluster, and the flywheel cheeks were fitted with steel side plates to boost crankcase compression

173cc BSA BANTAM D14/4

There can't be so very much wrong with a model which has held a solid place in the affections of the public for 20 years or more—and which is still a best-seller. Of course, the Bantam has changed a bit in that length of time; from a solid frame, through plunger rear springing to the current, orthodox pivoted rear fork, and from the initial 123 cc, through 148 cc to a healthy 173 cc.

Motor Cycle road test

And that is by no means the whole story. While growing up in size, it has acquired sophistication and a surprisingly big increase in power output. The long-lived three-speed gearbox has been replaced by a very welcome four-speed assembly, and instead of the former flywheel magneto and direct lighting there is a full alternator-rectifier-battery electrical system.

Minor improvements include a battery which can be kept in good order without the necessity for first detaching the dualseat, chromium-plated fuel-tank side panels, and two handlebar mirrors fitted as standard. Yet with all this the Bantam continues to be one of the best bargains on the British market, at just over £130. Quite an achievement.

Certainly it's a lightweight—it can be lifted about without trouble when, say, a narrow garden path has to be negotiated—but there is nothing tiddlerlike about the frame dimensions. The

Removal of the nearside panel reveals the battery and tool roll

SPECIFICATION

ENGINE: Capacity and type: 173 cc (61.5 x 58mm) two-stroke single. Bearings: Three ball mains, roller big-end. Lubrication: Petroil, 32 to 1 ratio. Mains lubricated from gear box and primary chaincase. Compression ratio: 10 to 1. Carburettor: Amal Concentric R626 (26mm choke). Air slide operated by handlebar lever. Mesh-and-felt air filter. Claimed output: 13 bhp at 5,750 rpm.

TRANSMISSION: Primary by $\frac{3}{8}$ x 0.250in chain in oilbath case; secondary by $\frac{1}{2}$in x 0.205in chain. Clutch: Multiplate. Overall gear ratios: 18.68, 12.04, 8.55 and 6.58 to 1. Engine rpm at 30 mph in top gear: 2,800.

ELECTRICAL EQUIPMENT: Ignition by 6-volt battery and coil, with emergency-start circuit. Charging: Wipac 60-watt alternator to 6-volt, 10-amp-hour battery through rectifier. Headlamp: Wipac 5in-diameter with 30/24-watt main bulb.

FUEL CAPACITY: $1\frac{7}{8}$ gallons.

TYRES: Dunlop Lightweight studded, 3.00 x 18in front and rear.

BRAKES: $5\frac{1}{2}$in diameter front and rear, with finger adjusters.

SUSPENSION: Hydraulically damped telescopic front fork. Pivoted rear fork controlled by Girling spring-and-hydraulic units.

DIMENSIONS: Wheelbase, 50in; ground clearance, $6\frac{1}{2}$in; seat height, 31in. All unladen.

WEIGHT: 215 lb dry.

PRICE: £130 16s 6d, including British purchase tax.

ROAD TAX: £5 a year.

MAKERS: BSA Motor Cycles Ltd, Armoury Road, Small Heath, Birmingham, 11.

PERFORMANCE

(Obtained by "Motor Cycle" staff at MIRA Proving Ground, Lindley, Leicestershire.)

MEAN MAXIMUM SPEED: 64 mph ($11\frac{1}{2}$-stone rider wearing two-piece trials suit and boots).

HIGHEST ONE-WAY SPEED: 66 mph (light, following three-quarter wind).

BRAKING: From 30 mph to rest on dry tarmac, 29ft 6in.

TURNING CIRCLE: 12ft 6in.

MINIMUM NON-SNATCH SPEED: 20 mph in top gear.

WEIGHT PER CC: 1.23 lb.

Following pages: the BSA Bantam was developed steadily over the years. The D14/4 led finally to the 1971 Bantam 175 pictured here (*National Motorcycle Museum*)

Midland Editor Bob Currie swings the Bantam through Birmingham's back streets

noticeable surge of energy as the revs start to climb from the lower end of the range, and this results in some very respectable acceleration figures—up to 50 mph, that is, for though there is plenty yet to come, it does mean squeezing the bottle to get it.

Keep the motor buzzing (and that's where the four-speed gearbox helps) and the Bantam will soar up a hill with complete contempt for the gradient. Of course, ye olde-tyme Bantam would get to the top, too, in its own sweet time—either by clinging doggedly to top cog until it was almost possible to count each rev, or by screaming along in second. The advantage of the new job lies not only in that well-chosen third gear, but also in the throaty, middle-of-the-range supply of urge.

A comfortable cruising speed turned out to be an indicated 60 mph (an actual 57 mph, allowing for speedometer error) but there was more to come, given only moderate encouragement. Running before the wind, it was possible to show slightly better than 70 mph on the dial at times.

Some slight roughness was evident at very low speeds in top gear. But this smoothed out from 30 mph, and in the middle reaches the power flow was as sweet as one could wish for.

Not thirsty

It is a recognised fact that the price of pepping-up a two-stroke is increased fuel consumption. Yet the Bantam is not especially thirsty. Keep it at 30 to 40 mph, and a return of 100 mpg is guaranteed—comforting news for those in search of a light, utterly reliable workhorse for city streets. Only if the throttle is held wide open does the fuel graph take a nose-dive.

The combination of light overall weight, nice balance, a nippy engine and precise steering showed up to the full when a particularly twisty length of B-class road was tackled. Cornering was limited only by the rather low (and non-adjustable) footrests. These are conditions a Bantam rider can enjoy. For although such roads have something less than billiard-table surfaces, the jolts and jars are not passed on to the man in the saddle, thanks to efficient fore and aft suspension.

The electrical system is 6-volt, yet this is quite adequate for the nature of the model, and a particularly good word should be given to the solid and handily-placed dipswitch toggle, easily operated by a gloved hand. As mentioned earlier, the battery has been made more accessible on the D14/4. It is secured by a spring toggle clamp, and may be extracted for in-

riding position is comfortable for both lankies and shorties, and though the 31 in seat height sounds a lot, the model's slimness allows the feet to be put down very confidently at halts.

An air lever is fitted to the handlebar, and for the first start of the morning best results were obtained when this was closed for a few seconds. At other times, it was quite sufficient just to tickle the carburettor.

Lower end

In gaining extra power output, the D14 Bantam has changed its characteristics in some degree, and it is no longer quite the low-speed slogger it used to be. There is a

Very much a two-up machine—a comfort-able dualseat, pillion foot-rests and power aplenty

spection and topping-up through an opening in the tool-box backplate, on the left. In theory, this is fine; in practice, extraction is hampered by the nearness of several loose cables draped across the opening.

Fasteners

One good point is the use of two half-turn Dzus fasteners to retain the tool-box lid, instead of the captive nuts which have exasperated a whole decade of Bantam owners. Another is the effective silencer with baffles which can be extracted for cleaning.

Finished in serviceable black (or blue)

Bottom-, second- and third-gear figures represent maximum-power revs, 8,000

Large enough for a 500 cc machine! The air-filter element is located behind a panel on the offside

with white lining on mudguards and tank and bright plated tank side-panels, the D14/4 Bantam is a smart little model which does credit to the long-honoured name. In terms of performance, it is far removed from the original D1 Bantam of 1948, but the family resemblance is unmistakable. And who's to say that there won't be a Bantam with us another 20 years from now?

The large-bore exhaust system just clears the frame's front down tube and protects the contact breaker low-tension lead from stone damage

| BOTTOM | SECOND | THIRD | TOP |

ACCELERATION

STANDING QUARTER-MILE Terminal Speed, 57 mph Time, 21·6 s

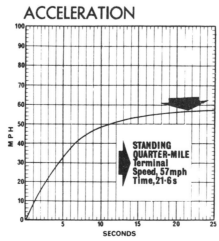

FUEL CONSUMPTION

BSA Victor Roadster

For a nippy little five-hundred roadster (a four-four-one initially, but it did grow into a full-blown five-hundred later) to be developed from a world championship-winning moto-cross model is a rare occurrence indeed. And where the Victor Roadster is concerned, that was only part of the story, for the tale began with a very humdrum little utility mount, the 249 cc C15.

In one sense, that first unit-construction BSA could be said to have been derived from the Edward Turner-designed 199 cc Triumph Tiger Cub (except that the cylinder was upright instead of inclined) and certainly there were strong family likenesses between the Cub and the C15 Star. As originally produced in 1959, the C15 produced a very modest 15 bhp at 7,000 rpm, but the initial roadster version was quickly followed by the C15S and C15T scrambles and trials models, and it was from these competitions variants that subsequent development took off.

Around 1960, Jeff Smith, Arthur Lampkin and one or two other riders were bounding about on C15s in the moto-cross field with considerable success, but it has to be said that by that time the bigger moto-cross BSA—the long-worshipped 500 cc Gold Star—was becoming outclassed in international competition. It was potent, but too heavy.

But could anything be done to upgrade the C15, ready to take over from the Goldie? The power was well down, of course, but on the other hand lightness and manoeuvrability would make up for that in part. BSA competitions manager Brian Martin began to experiment, and by taking a C15 barrel to the maximum bore it would stand (while keeping the stroke unchanged) he evolved a 343 cc model with which he had a blast at the 1961 Red Marley freak hill-climb.

Running on dope, the little bike zoomed up the slope to take both the 350 cc and unlimited capacity classes—an encouraging start, at the very least. The next step was to fit larger valves and carburettor, gorblimey cams and a high-compression piston. Jeff Smith took that one to Shrubland Park and ran rings round the opposition. And so was born the 343 cc B40, from which were derived a civilian roadster and a military model which was taken up by Britain and other NATO powers.

Now the B40 scrambler was fine for wiping up the 350 cc class, and also for adding 500 cc laurels if the opposition was not too strong. But even the great J. V. Smith found he was pushing his luck running it in international events. So by a little more juggling with bores and strokes an experimental 420 cc model was evolved, with which Smith gained first-time-out victory in the 1962 Hampshire Grand National.

So far, so good, but Jeff Smith was an exceptional character with a fine feeling for things mechanical, and in lesser hands the 420 cc tended to break up. The main trouble was that a lot more power was being pushed through what was still the soft-touring C15 gearbox. Designers Ernie Webster and Bert Curry got busy, and during the winter of 1963-4 devised a new version of the 420 cc moto-cross bike. The main changes included stronger, stub-toothed gear pinions in the gearbox, a more robust crankcase with ball and roller main bearings, a light-alloy cylinder barrel with chromium-plated bore—and an entirely new and lighter frame in which the main tube served as the oil reservoir.

Again Jeff gave it its first taste of battle in the Hants Grand National (this time the 1964 event), so collecting his fifth success in a row in that meeting. It soon became clear that BSA had a very tough little cookie indeed on their hands, and when the World Championship moto-cross rounds began Jeff packed the four-twenty into the back of his pick-up truck and headed for foreign parts. That summer, doing his own maintenance out in the field, he was to finish first in seven of the 14 races counting for Moto-Cross World Championship points, second in six more, and third in the remaining one—and even then the relatively lowly placing was due to a flat tyre.

As we have seen, a new and heftier crankcase had been evolved for Smith's model, and this encouraged the BSA design staff to go for still bigger things. The new casings allowed the bore and stroke to be pushed up to 79 × 90 mm, so producing a capacity of 441 cc. Again a model was made ready for Jeff Smith's sorties into the Moto-Cross World Championships. And again Jeff brought home the crown.

Translated into production terms, the machine became the

The Victor Roadster in an unusual setting. This one was being whanged around Brands Hatch by Alan Peck, prior to taking part in the Barcelona 24-Hour race

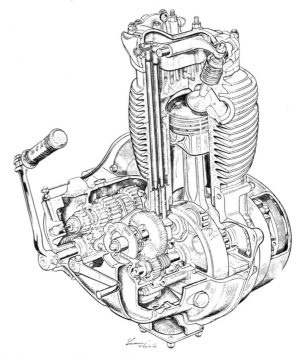

Ears muffled against the din, John Thickens puts a Grand Prix Victor engine through its paces on the test bench while Bob Currie looks on

B44 Victor MX, and a batch of Jeff Smith Replicas was prepared; here, the author can claim to have had a personal, if very modest, hand in things, for it was at his suggestion that the fuel tanks were painted in an eye-catching yellow—a distinct contrast with the nondescript finish of previous BSA scramblers.

The B44 Victor Roadster tested here was a surprise addition to the BSA parade at the 1966 Earls Court Show, with a 29 bhp power output which was almost double that of the modest little C15 from which it sprang.

Here, American readers may be slightly puzzled by reference to a Victor Roadster, because in the States the model was known from the outset as the B44SS Shooting Star (a name previously borne by a rather nice semi-sports A10 twin, in two-tone green). After only one year the Victor Roadster became the Shooting Star in Britain, too.

For 1969 the glass-fibre fuel tank was exchanged for a steel one with the same contours, on safety grounds, and a twin-leading-shoe front brake was employed. For 1970, there was a heavier-duty oil pump—a direct legacy of works participation in moto-cross.

But in the meantime, things had been happening on the moto-

On the titanium-frame BSA Victor MX, Jeff Smith forges ahead to win the Finnish Moto-Cross Grand Prix of 1966, near Helsinki. But the titanium frame had its drawbacks

Very far removed from its C15 remote ancestor was the 1966 B44 Victor unit, forged in the heat of world championship moto-cross. The light-alloy cylinder barrel had a chromium-plated bore. Present-day descendant is the Bolton-built CCM single

cross scene. In an expensive bid to hold the Moto-Cross World Championship title for a third year, BSA invested in a couple of all-titanium frames, but the effort was unsuccessful because these could not be repaired on site if fractures developed. A better proposition was the still further enlargement of the Victor engine, at first to 494 cc and finally to a full 499 cc. Headed by Jeff Smith and John Banks, the moto-cross team had a victorious televised winter series on the prototype B50 models, then launched into the summer events on the Continent with new frames built from Reynolds 531 tubing.

Nor was it only the off-road stuff. For several seasons, as part of the development programme, Tony Smith had been road-racing a BSA powered initially by a 343 cc, and later a 499 cc moto-cross engine, on the home circuits. Now came international glory, when a 499 cc B50 Shooting Star shared by Nigel Rollason and Clive Brown won, outright, the 1971 Spanish and Dutch 24-hour endurance marathons, and followed up with a sterling performance in the Bol d'Or.

Strictly speaking, the early 1970s are beyond the brief of this particular book, but to round off the story of the Victor family, the B44SS Shooting Star was eventually to give way to the B50SS Gold Star; the name was an unpardonable clanger by an unfeeling BSA publicity department, for of course the machine had no connection whatever with the immortal Goldies of the past. Styling went berserk, and the alleged Gold Star sported an indescribably ugly exhaust system with a black-painted almost-vertical lozenge silencer, a headlamp hung on bent wire, and short mudguards that might have been fine in Southern California but were ludicrous anywhere else.

But by mid-1972 BSA were in deep trouble, the run-down was well under way, and the company had only months to live. Right at the very end came one further, and unexpected development, when Cyril Halliburn put together a few experimental B50 speedway engines—BSA's first foray into this branch of the sport since 1930. The speedway BSA showed distinct promise, despite its shoestring-budget development, but closure of the factory brought it to an end before it had achieved full flowering.

ROAD TESTS OF NEW MODELS

441 cc BSA B44 Victor Roadster

WHEN the curtain rose on the 1966 BSA programme, there in the limelight stood something rather unexpected—a 441 cc roadster single. "But," spluttered the know-alls, "big singles went out years ago. These days it's got to be a twin, at least." Has it, now? They're not so daft at Small Heath and the Victor Roadster, taken all round, is a very logical machine. Logical as the ideal follow-on for the man graduating from a BSA two-fifty. Logical in giving the customer the benefit of all that Victor scrambler development.

Besides, the Victor represents a new conception in relatively big-capacity singles and is totally different from the heavyweights of the past. Note the 0.76 lb figure for weight per cc in the specification panel? That's the clue.

With its short wheelbase and high ground clearance, the frame has an obvious competition ancestry; the engine-gear lower-half assembly, too, is a direct result of moto-cross participation.

However, the 29 bhp of the engine is considerably less than the output of the grand-prix job. That means that the internals, built to take a bashing on the championship circuits, should be all but unburstable in everyday road use.

Where the Victor Roadster does differ most noticeably from the scrambles version is in the use of a square-finned, light-alloy cylinder barrel which gives it the appearance of a baby Gold Star.

With a hefty 7in ground clearance and a seat height of 31in, a rider does tend to be tall in the saddle and putting a foot down at traffic halts could mean something of a stretch for the short legged.

Above: The smart, cleanly styled Victor with square-finned barrel, high ground clearance and competition-proved bottom half. Right: Heart of the Victor, the power unit, developed for the tough world of scrambles, should prove unburstable in normal, everyday use

Left: Bob Currie samples the charms of the Victor. Above: Tool roll and battery are concealed behind the left-side faired panel. The key-operated ignition switch is to the left side of the carburettor

compression and the needle started to swing away from zero. At that, the trigger was released and one long swing of the pedal was enough to bring the engine to life.

Immediate realization is that useful power extends right down to the bottom of the rev range and that low-down punch is one of the Victor's greatest charms.

It permits the machine to get off the mark with all the urgency of an England forward streaking for a try; indeed, a little ham-fistedness in using the throttle and clutch could result in the front wheel pawing the air.

Shear heart, that's the phrase. Heart enough (as was proved while JON 119E was on duty at the Welsh Three-Day Trial) to tow a stranded competitor for 12 miles through the hills of mid-Wales. Heart enough to gallop gaily, two-up, over the switchback Tregaron pass.

Light as a model of only half its engine size, beautifully damped at front and rear and with brakes which would stop it on a sixpence, the Victor acts like a mechanized polo pony.

Lay it down, pick it up, spurt off again in a new direction . . . It could almost have been built with the corkscrews of the Tregaron in mind!

So it isn't a super-sportster? No, though an 87 mph maximum certainly doesn't indicate a slowcoach. Point is, a glamorous top speed isn't everything. The Victor's

Normally the model has an orthodox handlebar but it happens that the test machine was one diverted from an export batch, which explains the high-rising Western bar. Tastes vary, of course, but we found the high bend, in conjunction with the high seat, gave a remarkably comfortable and controllable ride of sit-up-and-beg style.

TECHNIQUE

Starting-up may mean, for some, the recall of an almost forgotten technique; for others, new to a largish-capacity single, it is something to be learned. First thing to remember is that this is a high-compression engine and the exhaust-valve lifter, on the left side of the bar, is no mere ornament.

Best plot was to switch on and watch the ammeter needle. With the exhaust-lift trigger pulled up, the starter pedal was pushed down gently until the piston was eased over

handleability through corners and rapid acceleration out of them will get it places quicker than some of the hotted-up glamour irons.

The turning circle is unusually small and with that amount of bottom-end poke you can have fun chuntering around in ever-decreasing circles doing a fair impression of Sammy Miller. On the road it is a shade light at the front end but that is a BSA characteristic which soon becomes accepted.

Clutch operation was sweet and gave no cause for complaint even after a series of violent acceleration tests. Put

that together with a delightfully smooth and utterly clash-free gear change and you have a model which is a joy to ride.

At the current speed limit of 70 mph the engine is running particularly smoothly and happily; though some vibration can be felt through the tank on the way up there, it is never enough to be uncomfortable.

Talking of the fuel tank, this is in glass-fibre and very pleasantly styled but its capacity of a bare two gallons is on the meagre side—all right

for the Americans, perhaps, using the bike for a spot of weekend enjoyment but for Britain something larger would be appreciated.

That goes for the rear chain, too: $\frac{5}{8} \times \frac{1}{4}$in is hardly man enough for a 441 cc model and it had to be adjusted several times during the test.

To get all the moans over at once (and none of them is very serious), while the glass-fibre tool-box cover comes off readily enough, the space provided for the tool roll is barely adequate.

The electrics earned high marks. Even the horn note

was amply penetrating, while the beam of the 12-volt, 50-watt headlamp made night riding a real pleasure.

The dipped beam was flat-topped and didn't appear to offend oncoming drivers but the dipswitch was sluggish in action and on several occasions caused both main-bulb filaments to light at once.

Accentuated by the light-alloy cylinder, piston slap was evident when the engine was cold but dwindled to an acceptable level as the Victor warmed to its work.

The same could not be said of the exhaust, however; that was definitely crisp at the best

Above: Diverted from the export line, this model is fitted with a high-style handlebar. Our tester found it comfortable. Left: That bar from a different angle. And this view emphasizes the neat lines of the glass-fibre tank with its quick-action filler cap

of times and rose to a bark when the throttle was opened hard.

Finally, some little points worth mentioning. The quickly detachable rear wheel really is good and comes out without trouble in less than a minute. Sensibly placed under the steering head, the Zener diode is on a finned, light-alloy mounting which receives a healthy cooling blast.

The oil tank cap has an attached dipstick—but *don't* fill the tank to the top mark, or oil will spill out of the froth-tower breather. (A revised marking will be used on later models.)

Overall impressions? A zippy, handy model which bids fair to give the big single a new lease of life. Those who have never tried the type before are in for a very pleasant surprise.

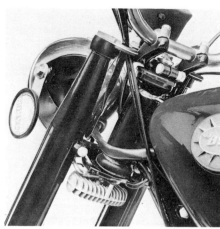

SPECIFICATION

ENGINE
Capacity and type: 441 cc (79 x 90 mm) overhead-valve single.
Bearings: Roller drive-side and ball timing-side mains; double-row roller big-end.
Lubrication: Dry sump; tank capacity, 4 pints.
Compression ratio: 9.4 to 1.
Carburettor: Amal Concentric, type 930/1 30mm choke. No air slide.
Gauze and wire-mesh air filter.
Claimed output: 29 bhp at 5,750 rpm.

TRANSMISSION
Primary: ⅜in duplex chain.
Secondary: ⅝ × ¼in chain.
Clutch: Multi-plate.
Gear ratios: 13.38, 8.33, 6.32 and 5.05 to 1.
Engine rpm at 30 mph in top gear, 2,000.

ELECTRICAL EQUIPMENT
Ignition: Battery and coil.
Charging: Lucas 100-watt alternator to 12-volt, ten-amp-hour battery through rectifier.
Headlamp: 6½in-diameter with 50/40-watt main bulb.

FUEL CAPACITY: 2 gallons.
TYRES: Dunlop K70 3.25 × 18 ribbed front, 3.50 × 18in studded rear.
BRAKES: 7in diameter front and rear; finger adjusters.
SUSPENSION: BSA telescopic front fork with hydraulic damping. Pivoted rear fork controlled by Girling spring-and-hydraulic units; three-position adjustment for load.
DIMENSIONS: Wheelbase, 52in; ground clearance, 7in; seat height, 31in. All unladen.
WEIGHT: 336 lb, including one gallon of petrol.
PRICE: £281 14s, including British purchase tax.
ROAD TAX: £8 a year. £2 19s for four months.
MAKERS: BSA Motor Cycles, Ltd, Armoury Road, Small Heath, Birmingham, 11.

PERFORMANCE

(Obtained by "Motor Cycle" staff at the Motor Industry Research Association's proving ground, Lindley, Leicestershire)
MEAN MAXIMUM SPEED: 87 mph (11-stone rider wearing two-piece suit).
HIGHEST ONE-WAY SPEED: 90 mph (light following wind).
BRAKING: From 30 mph to rest on dry tarmac, 30 ft.
TURNING CIRCLE: 13ft 9in.
MINIMUM NON-SNATCH SPEED: 18 mph in top gear.
WEIGHT PER CC: 0.76 lb.

441 cc BSA B44 VICTOR ROADSTER

Bottom-, second-, and third-gear figures represent maximum-power revs, 5,750

BOTTOM

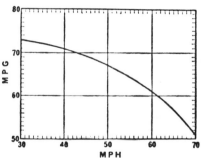

SECOND

THIRD

TOP

FUEL CONSUMPTION

ACCELERATION

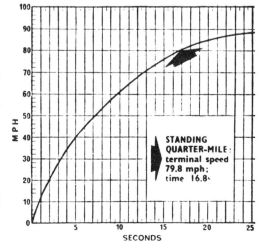

STANDING QUARTER-MILE: terminal speed 79.8 mph; time 16.8

Triumph TR25W Trophy

As the opening sentence of the road test makes clear, there was very little about the TR25W Triumph Trophy that was 'Triumph'—except the familiar die-cast 'eyebrow'-type tank badges and the Tiger 90 front fork. In other respects the machine was pure-bred Small Heath, and its ancestry can be traced to the first unit-construction C15 BSA of 1959. So before we get too deep into the tale, let us settle the matter of the actual capacity of the engine. Bore and stroke dimensions were 67×70 mm, which gives a capacity of 247 cc, but almost throughout the life of the C15 and its progeny the BSA Group advertised it as being 249 cc. Not until right at the end, with the 1971 BSA B25SS Gold Star, Triumph Trail Blazer, and others, did the literature admit to 247 cc.

So why the deception? BSA once told me that it was because their first-ever two-fifty, the 1924 'Round Tank', was 249 cc and they wanted to preserve continuity. Well, perhaps; but there was also the fact that the purchaser of a 249 cc would feel he was getting 2 cc more for his money!

Anyway, development of the original C15 began almost immediately, with much help from the competitions department and their ace moto-cross men of the day, Jeff Smith and Arthur Lampkin. Two moto-cross C15s were prepared, for Jeff and Arthur to ride in the 1960 European Championships series, and from experience gained in this way the roadster C15 was given steel instead of cast-iron flywheels for 1961.

In time, it inherited ball and roller main bearings (instead of plain and ball), needle-roller gearbox layshaft bearings, and various other goodies. The cooking C15 acquired, too, a more sporty companion in the C15 Sport Star SS80—a cheeky piece of naming which must have caused many an old Brough

The TR25W Trophy was essentially the BSA B25 in slightly different dress, and with lower overall gearing. Here is the 1967 BSA Barracuda, later renamed Starfire, and finally Gold Star 250

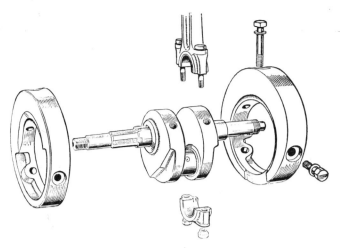

Unusual crankshaft assembly of the Triumph TR25W. The shaft was a one-piece forging, the separate flywheels being secured by radial bolts. The method of construction dictated the use of a steel-backed shell big-end bearing

Superior fancier to choke over his bread-and-milk.

But the big revamp was yet to come. While the C15 title pointed to what was originally a 15 bhp engine, the introduction in November, 1966, of the B25 Barracuda was rather more than a big jump in power output to 25 bhp at 8,000 rpm. While the general configuration appeared much as before, there were totally new crankcases, housing for the first time a one-piece forged crankshaft to the webs of which were fixed (by radial bolts in twin-cylinder style) a pair of separate flywheel rings. An added bonus of this arrangement, incidentally, was that if heavier flywheels were required for a trials version, or skimpier wheels for a grasser, the conversion was quite simple.

Other details included a duralumin connecting rod, and a steel-backed shell big-end bearing replaced the former caged-roller fitment. There was a revised lubrication system, and a new square-looking light-alloy cylinder barrel. The sculptured fuel tank was in glassfibre (at this stage, nobody had yet raised doubts about the safety of such a tank) and, all in all, the Barracuda was claimed to be 'Britain's fastest production 250'—although Royal Enfield, whose Continental GT was a usefully nippy device, would no doubt query the statement. Certainly the Barracuda did not feature very strongly in 250 cc

End of the line for the BSA/Triumph 250 cc unit was the Gold Star 250 SS of 1971. Triumph equivalent was the Trail Blazer, styling being almost identical. Sump undershield, and fork-pivot chain adjustment were inherited from moto-cross

production-machine racing, although the engine did make a considerable impact in grass-tracking, when installed in suitable frames by Hagon, Elstar, or Antig.

The BSA Barracuda sounded a nicely alliterative name, but it would appear that Small Heath had not done its homework properly, because there was already a Barracuda of somebody else's make (Bridgestone, was it?) on the USA market. After a rethink, BSA announced that from April, 1968 the B25 would be known as the Starfire. And just to make it a little bit different, it would have a full-width front hub.

A little later a Fleetstar version (in black and white) was added, for institutional purposes—police, gas board, courier agencies, etc. And the glassfibre tank gave way to one of identical outward appearance, but made in steel, with anodised-light-alloy badges.

First news of the Triumph TR25W came from the USA, where the model was launched in January, 1968, basically as a trail bike and therefore featuring lower overall gear ratios than its BSA counterpart, in addition to a high-level exhaust pipe on the right. Its European debut was to have been at the Amsterdam Show, a month later, but due to a mix-up it was held up by Dutch customs officials, and never reached the exhibition.

On the British market, the TR25W Trophy (rather an unfortunate choice of name as there was already a 650 cc Trophy in the Triumph programme) had its official launch in October, 1968, replacing the long-lived and much-loved Tiger Cub in the Meriden line up. But in fact supplies had been sneaking into the showrooms for a month or so before that, as witness the 4 September test of the model.

Incidentally, whatever happened to the 'TOP 20' registration when the BSA-Triumph Group went to the wall? Any aspiring disc jockey would have given his eye teeth to acquire it.

The next change in the little Triumph was in April, 1970, when the high-level exhaust was switched to the left side of the bike for no good reason. Indeed, it was now far less tucked-in than before, in consequence of which it had to be provided with a glassfibre heat shield, and that cannot have done much to improve riding comfort.

For 1971 came another major revamp, although this time the power unit was largely untouched. Instead, it was dropped into what was really a production edition of the works moto-cross frame, complete with oil-carrying top and front-down frame tubes. Also inherited from the moto-cross mounts was a pivoted rear fork with eccentric pivot mounting, so that the entire fork moved rearward to adjust the chain, thereby keeping the wheel in line. A rather doubtful change was an ugly-looking lozenge silencer, rising at the rear of the seat sub-frame tube to discharge at high level. The silencer itself was dull black, albeit decorated with a polished and perforated cover plate. For the rest, all the usual Umberslade Hall excesses were evident—vestigial mud-guards, bare fork stanchions, headlamp carried on bent wire brackets. Even they might have been forgiven by loyal BSA fans, in time. But nobody could possibly forgive the change of name from Starfire to 'Gold Star', so sullying the memory of a machine which had *earned* such a title.

By now, any differences that had existed between the Triumph and BSA two-fifties had been abandoned, and only the tank badges offered any distinction. BSA had the B25T Victor Trail at £337; Triumph countered with the TR25W Trail Blazer at the same price. Equivalent roadsters were the BSA B25R Gold Star, and Triumph TR25 Blazer SS, each at £312. But neither would survive for much longer, in the economic blizzard sweeping down on Small Heath.

249cc TRIUMPH TROPHY

Nobody's trying to kid anybody, so to get the record straight from the start let's confirm that—apart from the Triumph name on the rocker-box cover and the primary-chaincase motif—the engine-gear unit of the 249 cc Triumph Trophy is identical in every way with the equivalent model, the Starfire, in the BSA range.

Motor Cycle road test

Strictly speaking, the new Triumph is a USA-style trail bike, intended for pottering about in the mountains. That accounts for the big tyres ($3 \cdot 25 \times 19$ in front, $4 \cdot 00 \times 18$ in rear), crankcase undershield, high-level exhaust and small trials silencer, ISDT-pattern headlamp and generally up-in-the-air build.

It accounts, too, for the lowish overall gearing. Similarity with the Starfire ends at the gearbox, and from there on the Triumph wears 15-tooth gearbox and 52-tooth rear-wheel sprockets, as against the BSA's 16-tooth and 49-tooth arrangement. As a quick check, that gives a bottom ratio of 20·79 to 1 (Starfire, 18·3 to 1) and top gear of 7·84 to 1 (Starfire, 6·91 to 1).

Apart from the mechanical differences, there is the matter of styling which, in some subtle way, really does give the newcomer a Meriden air. The fuel tank is steel (and holds a useful 3¾ gallons), the dualseat has the now-familiar Triumph cross-ribbed top; and there are typically Triumph sports mudguards, plus attractive—if somewhat angular—glassfibre covers to the tool box and oil tank.

Though versions of the TR25W being sent to the USA have Dunlop Trials Universal tyres fore and aft, models now reaching the British market have—in deference to British tastes—road-going Dunlop K70s instead.

But before going on—how about that registration number TOP 20? It's a publicity gimmick, of course, and a good one at that.

The story behind it is that the Lord Mayor of Birmingham, on a recent tour of the factory, happened to remark that his son owned a clapped-out 1965 Tiger Cub bearing that number. Not slow on the uptake, Triumph bought the old Cub, scrapped it and, for £5, had TOP 20 transferred to the new bike.

Now for the test. Get astride the model and you certainly feel a long way off the deck; touching the ground is a tip-toe affair for anyone of average leg length. It's understandable, for to get the 8-in ground clearance required for mountain trail work, the seat height has been pushed up to 32 in.

For that reason, the high-rise handlebar is something of a necessity if a comfortable riding stance is adopted.

With you up there and the bike somewhere down below, there is the feeling that you can swing the little Triumph about between your knees. You can. There's nothing which can ground, not even a centre stand.

Some may look askance at the fat and studded front Dunlop, much preferring a ribbed job for tarmac. Nevertheless, the steering seemed perfectly acceptable.

Since we road-tested the Starfire (or Barracuda, as it was then), the Amal Monobloc is out, and the Concentric is in, even on Triumphs. No air slide is fitted to the little Trophy, and the odd thing is that it doesn't appear to appreciate a cold-start carb flood.

Turn on the juice, just a light touch of the float tickler, no more; and the engine fires, first kick, as like as not. With the engine hot, omit the tickle and it is still a first-time starter.

Spot on

Carburation was spot on with the revs climbing cleanly up the scale as the throttle was opened. and the fuel-consumption graph was impressive; over 100 miles to the gallon at a steady 30 mph is a creditable effort.

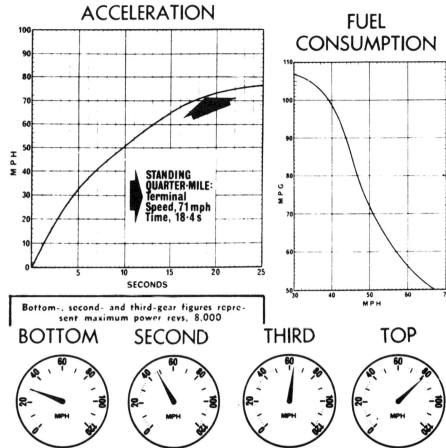

ACCELERATION

STANDING QUARTER-MILE:
Terminal Speed, 71 mph
Time, 18·4 s

FUEL CONSUMPTION

Bottom-, second- and third-gear figures represent maximum power revs, 8,000

BOTTOM   SECOND   THIRD   TOP

Following pages: Dave Griffith's Triumph TR25W Trophy, which has non-standard Metal Profiles front fork and Royal Enfield front wheel (*Bob Currie*)

The all-round lowering of the gear ratios is noticeable straight away, and the net effect is to produce an immensely likeable model for town and around. No need to wring its neck before getting into the next notch up; the revs come freely and the acceleration is slick.

At least, it would be, if it wasn't for the piffling little silencer. Sure enough, there is a mute in the end of the tail pipe, but it still emits an embarrasingly loud bark; and that rather takes the edge off the fun of giving the bike full rein.

How does the low top gear affect the flat-out performance? Not so much as might be expected. Triumph don't put the Trophy 250 forward as a speedster (if you must have that little bit extra of top

Only the name on the rocker box identifies the timing side of the power unit from that of the 250 cc BSA engine

whack, there's always the BSA Starfire) and they were most surprised when David Dixon—in racing leathers admittedly—whammed through the MIRA speed trap at 81 mph mean. They'd geared it to do only 78!

To answer the unspoken question, bulkier Bob Currie clocked a two-way 75 mph; which probably proves something or other. Dixon's comment? 'Smashing little bike!'

If you think you've spotted a Tiger 90 front fork on the machine, you're dead right. There is a beautiful action to the front end, smooth and controlled in both directions, with hardly ever a clash; but softer rear springing would have been an improvement. Even with 14½ stones aboard, and the dampers in the softest of the three settings, the Triumph tended to hop about on roughish going.

A 5½-in diameter headlamp doesn't seem adequate but at least there is full 12-

volt lighting (with the diode nicely out in the cooling air, underneath the lamp) and the main beam turned out to be a surprisingly good one, ample for a night-time 60 mph gallop.

It is the type of headlamp evolved for ISDT machines, and has a push-and-push-again dip button in the top of the shell; not the ideal arrangement for a quick dip at dead of night, but effective, none the less.

There is no denying the TR25W Trophy is a smart little job in its flamboyant red finish and it is likely to create a lot of interest as news of it starts to spread around.

During the time it was in *Motor Cycle's* hands it was used for weekend reporting of various meetings and, invariably, spectators flocked round wherever it was parked.

Their verdict was an echo of David Dixon's. A smashing little bike. It is, too!

SPECIFICATION ··

ENGINE: Capacity and type 249 cc (67 x 70mm) overhead-valve single Bearings; two ball journal mains, plain big end Lubrication dry sump, capacity, 6 pints Compression ratio: 10 to 1. Carburettor Amal Concentric 928, with gauze-and-mesh air filter. No air slide Claimed output 25 bhp at 8,000 rpm.
TRANSMISSION: Primary ⅜in duplex chain in oilbath case Secondary ⅜ x ¼in chain Clutch multi-plate Gear ratios 7.94, 9.75, 12.9 and

20.79 to 1. Engine rpm at 30 mph in top gear, 3,100.
ELECTRICAL EQUIPMENT: Ignition battery and coil. Charging Lucas 110-watt alternator through rectifier and Zener diode to 12-volt, 10-amp-hour battery Headlamp Lucas 5½in-diameter with 50/40-watt main bulb.
FUEL CAPACITY: 3¼ gallons
TYRES: Dunlop K70 studded 3.25 x 19in front, 4.00 x 18in rear
BRAKES: 7in-diameter front and rear, with finger adjusters

SUSPENSION: Hydraulically damped telescopic front fork, pivoted rear fork controlled by Girling spring-and-hydraulic units with three-position load adjustment
DIMENSIONS: Wheelbase 53in, ground clearance, 8in, seat height, 32in All unladen
WEIGHT: 320 lb dry
PRICE: £269 19s 10d including British purchase tax.
ROAD TAX: £5 a year
MAKERS: Triumph Engineering Co Ltd, Meriden Works, Allesley Coventry

PERFORMANCE

(Obtained by "Motor Cycle" staff at the Motor Industry Research Association's proving ground, Lindley, Leicestershire.)
MEAN MAXIMUM SPEED: 81 mph (11½-stone rider wearing racing leathers)
HIGHEST ONE-WAY SPEED: 84 mph (fresh three-quarter wind)
BRAKING: From 30 mph to rest on dry tarmac, 30ft
TURNING CIRCLE: 13ft 6in
MINIMUM NON-SNATCH SPEED: 16 mph in top gear
WEIGHT PER CC: 1.29 lb

Norton Commando

To the outside observer (and probably to the inside observer, too!) the final days of the once-great AMC combine seemed wrapped in utter confusion, and the production programme—if it could be dignified by that name—comprised a sleight-of-hand trick by which Matchless engines appeared in Norton frames, and vice-versa. But at least there was a Norton-engined Norton, too, and it does have direct relevance to this particular tale, because this was the 745 cc (73 × 89 mm bore and stroke) Atlas vertical twin, developed at Woolwich after the close-down of Norton's Bracebridge Street home, and introduced initially in 1965 for export markets and (hopefully) for home police duty.

By August, 1966, AMC was in liquidation. Yet some sort of salvation was just around the corner, for now Dennis Poore and his Manganese Bronze Holdings company came upon the scene. Manganese was the parent group of the Wolverhampton-based Villiers engine firm, and now Poore stepped in, to scoop up some of the old AMC assets from the liquidator, in particular the Norton, Matchless, and AJS manufacturing rights (although the kiss of death was given to James and Francis-Barnett, the remaining members of the former AMC family).

Under the new banner of Norton-Villiers Ltd (Norton-Matchless division), the Woolwich works re-opened, with a still further abbreviated programme of which the 745 cc Norton unit was still very much a part. There was the Matchless-framed Atlas, plus a USA-market version of the Atlas in a light, scrambles-type frame; this was the P11, later known as the Ranger.

Meanwhile, in January, 1967, Dr. Stephan Bauer had joined Norton-Villiers from Rolls-Royce, and in association with former AMC designer Bob Trigg and Villiers designer Bernard Hooper, began work on a new machine with a new concept in frame design.

The result was unveiled at the Earls Court Show held in September, 1967, and certainly stole the scene. It was, of course, the Commando, which combined the 745 cc Norton Atlas engine (installed with the cylinder block canted forward) with a totally new and light frame based on a 2¼-in diameter backbone tube through which passed all frame stresses; two subsidiary triangulated tubes gave resistance to twisting.

The most revolutionary feature of the Commando was that the engine, gearbox, and rear fork formed an independent sub-frame, held to the main frame by three rubber mountings. Engine and road vibration were, therefore, contained in the sub-assembly and not passed to the rider. Rather surprisingly, the opportunity was not taken to adopt unit construction, and instead the engine and gearbox remained separate, with the rear fork pivoted from the gearbox mounting plates.

Styling of the machine was ultra-modern, and embodied a 3½ gallon fuel tank in glassfibre (still an acceptable material for the purpose at that time) with a 'fastback' tail of the same material.

Unused to the world of motor cycle manufacture, Norton-Villiers had expended much gold in commissioning a 'house image' from a London agency—and the outcome was what the public came to know as the 'dreaded green blob', a circular green tank badge which reflected the similar device used on the firm's letter-heading.

Although the blob appeared on the Earls Court Show machines—it did not include the Norton name, which had, perforce, to be added to the tank separately—it had been dropped by the time the first production Commandos appeared on the home market in May, 1968.

That the new Norton had production-racing potential was soon evident, a Commando prepared by Paul Dunstall and ridden by Ray Pickrell claiming a first-time-out victory in the 750 cc class of the Isle of Man Production-machine TT race. That was just the start, and from that point on Commandos were seen in production-class racing in ever-growing numbers.

However, the days of the Woolwich works were numbered, and the very last Commandos left the line there in July, 1969. The new arrangement was that engines would be built at the former Villiers works in Marston Road, Wolverhampton, and shipped down by road to Andover, where Norton-Villiers had acquired brand-new premises on a trading estate. It seemed an

July, 1969, and all motor cycle production at the Woolwich works came to an end. Last bike off the line was this Commando; later models were built first at Andover, and finally at Wolverhampton

The Norton Commando engine was to become almost universal in sidecar moto-cross, this Wasp outfit (raced by Bill Jukes) being typical of the breed

odd arrangement, but the cost of transporting engines from Wolverhampton (and frames from the Reynolds Tube factory in Birmingham) to Andover could be offset by the grant obtainable from Andover corporation—or something like that, anyway.

Announced later the same year, the 1970 Norton range included the Commando 'S', a USA-styled model with twin high-level exhausts. For home enthusiasts, there was cheering news that the dreaded green blob had gone for good and, instead, the old traditional Norton name-style was back on the tank in good and readable lettering (even better news was to follow, when a Commando in black, with gold tank lining, was made available for 1971).

On the racing side, victories continued to pile up, and mention should be made of the Thruxton 500-miler win in 1970 by Peter Williams and Charlie Sanby, because Peter was to play a big part in the Norton days yet to come. Right at the end of the year, Norton-Villiers announced their 1971 plans and, strictly speaking, the Commando story from that point on should be outside the brief of this particular book.

All the same, that 1971 programme is interesting, containing as it did the basic Commando Fastback, plus the Roadster (the one with black-and-gold tank), Commando SS, semi-chopper Hi-Rider, and for police work, the Interpol. Detail improvements included a quickly-detachable rear wheel with inbuilt transmission shock absorber, and a modified front fork with reduced trail and sealed and non-adjustable head bearings. New

Main feature of the Commando frame was a large-diameter top tube. The rear fork was pivoted from the gearbox mounting plates, and the whole engine and gearbox sub-assembly was rubber mounted

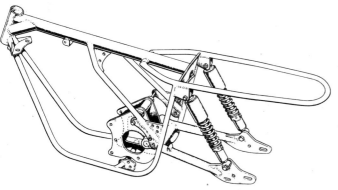

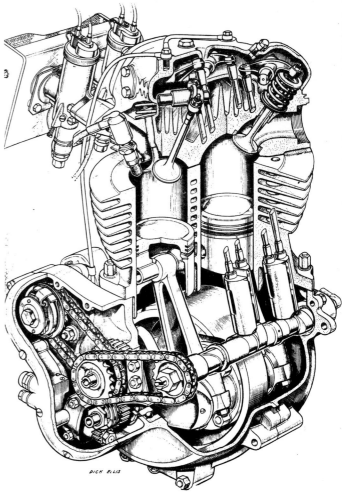

Origin of the Commando engine was the 745 cc Norton Atlas, here seen with details laid bare. The first Commandos used the Atlas engine in an inclined instead of vertical position in the frame

silencers with long reverse-cone outlets tamed the noise output to 82 decibels.

Much would happen to the Commando as the 1970s got under way. There would be a new racing team, managed by Frank Perris, led by Peter Williams, and sponsored by tobacco kingpins, John Player. Production of the Norton as a whole would be transferred to Wolverhampton. The engine would grow up to 850 cc and, in the Mk. III version for 1976, adopt electric starting.

But 1976 would also bring liquidation for the Norton-Villiers section of what, by then, had become the Norton-Villiers-Triumph group. Then, too, the closure of Wolverhampton would promote a Meriden-style sit-in—and, at one stage, the possibility of salvation by Lord Hesketh, although that was not to become fact.

At the time of writing, the Norton name is alive and well at Shenstone, Staffs, where final development work is being completed on the Wankel-powered model that will take Norton into the 1980s. But that is not the Commando; apart from a few assembled at Andover from stock parts, the Commando died when the Wolverhampton factory gates were closed.

745cc NORTON COMMANDO

No new model introduced in the past decade has made such a big impact as the Norton Commando. It was first seen at the London Show last September and greeted with enthusiasm, though in some cases the welcome was reserved until production machines were available.

Motor Cycle road test

They were ready in May and experience on the road showed that the Norton marque had come back with a bang. The terrific power of the modified 745 cc Atlas twin was a new experience now it was rubber-mounted in an ingenious frame which did, in fact, virtually eliminate the effects of high-frequency vibration.

The sceptics retired to swallow their doubts. Overnight the Commando became the most-sought-after large-capacity roadster on the market.

Something more exhaustive than an orthodox road test was called for if the full potential of this bike was to be assessed. Thus TYT 63F was flown across the Channel in July after the routine performance figures had been obtained at the MIRA proving ground.

To say that the Commando showed up well would be grudging praise. In a 2,000-mile trip it proved a distance-devourer *par excellence*. Yet it was equally satisfying to ride in heavy traffic; on byroads in Italy and Switzerland, and high on alpine passes. It gave a new dimension to the sort of riding we have known on parallel twins in the past 20 years.

In short, the Commando provides an over-115 mph maximum speed, an acceleration graph like the side of a house, relatively light fuel consumption at high cruising speeds, woofling docility when required and a riding position that ensures complete comfort. All this, with a commendably low level of mechanical and exhaust noise.

At home

The basic Atlas engine is no newcomer. Its Commando application involved far more than installing it with a forward inclination in rubber mountings. Much development work has been completed. While it retains its capacity for producing beefy torque at low revolutions it is equally at home revving freely at

6,800 rpm and pushing out nearly 60 bhp.

In fact, with the standard 19-tooth gear-box sprocket fitted, the maximum speed of 117 mph obtained equals 7,200 rpm. The engine has ample margins and revs of this order are completely safe, but a 21-tooth sprocket is available if preferred. For high-speed riding it is, in practice, rarely necessary to exceed 5,000 rpm in any gear. The spread of power is so wide that, for example, a whiff

The comfortable riding position and taut feel of the Commando enable it to be ridden with satisfying verve on twisty roads

of throttle in top gear moves the speedometer needle very smartly from, say, 75 to 100 mph—invaluable when mile-eating on the fast, though far-from-straight, major roads in eastern France.

With such an ample supply of power, pass storming in the Alps was a really enjoyable exercise. Gradient and traffic baulks could be dealt with by the zippy yet unobtrusive acceleration.

Less orthodox

It was no hardship to use the indirect gears when necessary. The ratios are happily chosen and could be engaged rapidly and positively—from third to top as easily and quietly without clutch operation as with it.

The clutch is one of the Commando's less orthodox features. It has a diaphragm (with four friction plates) and is capable of dealing with more torque than the earlier, coil-spring clutch. It takes up the drive a shade more quickly but, apart from that, is better in every way. It proved light to operate, freed completely at all times and showed no signs of slipping or becoming overheated.

Handling is well up to the traditional Norton standards. The Commando has that taut, manageable feel at all speeds that encourages clean, stylish cornering. It keeps on line, can be flicked confidently through close-coupled S-bends and does not waver when banked over on bumpy surfaces.

The silencers limit banking angle but not to an unrealistic extent. Side and centre stands are well tucked away though they are slightly difficult to reach and push down with the foot.

Slight flutter

Steering is rock steady at all speeds above about 40 mph. Below that, there is slight handlebar flutter if the hands are re-

moved from the grips. It is unnoticed in normal circumstances and might never be apparent unless the no-hands test is made.

The twin-leading-shoe front brake was, as expected, excellent, but the single-leading-shoe rear brake lacked power and occasionally failed to free properly. On the whole, braking was satisfactory (31 ft from 30 mph) but no more.

As mentioned earlier, the rider is well insulated from engine vibration. This factor alone is a comfort boost, especially on a 400-plus daily mileages such as undertaken during the text. But there is more to Commando comfort than this.

The riding position—the placing of the seat, handlebar grips, footrests and

Inclined forward in the new frame, the 745 cc, twin-cylinder Atlas engine packs beefy power right through the range

controls—is spot on and the only possible criticism might be that the well-padded dualseat, at 31 in from ground level, is a bit high for some riders.

Starting was invariably easy—usually one prod on the pedal was enough. With the engine cold the only difference was to close the air lever. With next-to-no warming up, the engine would idle re-

The Commando has a completely new frame layout yet retains the powerful, thoroughbred lines long associated with high-performance Nortons

liably at only a shade over 600 rpm. Despite much hard riding, the twin Amal Concentric carburettors retained their slow-running settings and balance.

The electrical side, too, was faultless. During the continental trip it proved to be properly weatherproofed. The bike was usually parked in the open and on one occasion it was ridden for 10 hours in continuous rain. The engine never missed a beat.

Lighting permitted 80-mph cruising in the dark. A much-appreciated practical feature is the easily-operated toggle switch in the headlamp shell. Very useful, too, is the headlamp-flasher button in the dipswitch/horn console on the left side of the handlebar.

Another practical feature is the rear-chain oiler. It kept the chain lightly lubricated without surplus oil reaching the wall of the tyre. The chain needed adjustment at approximately 800-mile intervals.

Over the long continental mileage, some of it at high cruising speeds, the fuel consumption worked out at a shade over 50 mpg—lighter than usual with some machines of smaller capacity. Premium-type fuel, 98 octane, was used. The engine could be made to pink on this fuel but not seriously enough to warrant a higher-octane diet.

Oil consumption was 300 miles to the pint. This is thought to be higher than average but there was no obvious explanation. The exhaust was not smoky and the engine remained free from serious leaks.

Accessibility for servicing is good. A quickly detachable panel on the left below the seat nose reveals the battery.

Staffman Peter Fraser, who used the Commando for his visit to the ISDT venue at San Pellegrino in Italy, refuelling on his way back across France

745 cc NORTON COMMANDO

Bottom-, second- and third-gear figures represent maximum - power revs, 6,800

ACCELERATION

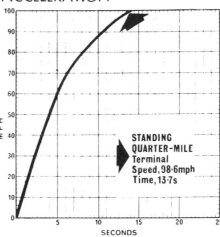

STANDING QUARTER-MILE Terminal Speed, 98·6mph Time, 13·7s

FUEL CONSUMPTION

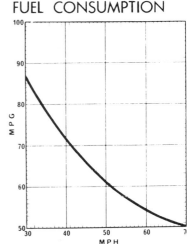

The seat itself can be removed in seconds without spanners. Tools are stored in a compartment in the glass-fibre tail fairing.

A single-bolt fixing for the cast-aluminium primary chain-case makes inspection and servicing unusually easy.

The Commando has set a new high in the field of big-capacity machines for which Britain has been famous for so long. It deserves the welcome it received when production started and the big reputation it is building now more and more machines are reaching world markets.

specification

ENGINE: Capacity and type: 745 cc (73 x 89mm) overhead-valve, parallel twin. Bearings: crankshaft supported in a roller bearing on the drive side and a ball bearing on the timing side; plain big ends and small ends. Lubrication: dry sump; oil-tank capacity, 5 pints. Compression ratio: 8.9 to 1. Carburettors: twin Amal Concentric, 30mm-diameter choke; air slides operated by handlebar lever. Impregnated-paper air-filter element. Claimed power output: 58 bhp at 6,800 rpm.
TRANSMISSION: Primary by ⅜in. triplex chain with movable gear box for adjustment; secondary by ⅝ x ⅜in chain. Clutch: multi-plate, with diaphram-spring. Gear ratios: 12.4, 8.25, 5.9, 4.84 to 1. Engine rpm at 30 mph in top gear: 1,850.
ELECTRICAL EQUIPMENT: Ignition by capacitor and twin coils. Charging by 110-watt alternator through rectifier and diode to 8-amp-hour battery. Headlamp: 7in-diameter, with 50/40-watt main bulb.
FUEL CAPACITY: 3¼ gallons.
BRAKES: 8in-diameter, twin-leading-shoe front; 7in-diameter rear
TYRES: Avon ribbed front, 3.00 x 19in; Avon GP rear, 3.50 x 19in.
SUSPENSION: Norton Roadholder telescopic fork with two-way hydraulic damping; pivoted rear fork controlled by Girling spring-and-hydraulic units with three-position adjustment for load.
DIMENSIONS: Wheelbase, 56¾in; ground clearance, 6in; seat height, 31in, all unladen.
WEIGHT: 418 lb, including half a gallon of fuel and full oil tank.
PRICE: £456 19s 4d, including British purchase tax.
ROAD TAX: £10 a year; £3 13s for four months.
MANUFACTURERS: Norton Villiers Ltd, Norton Matchless Division, 44 Plumstead Road, London, SE18.

performance

(Obtained by "Motor Cycle" staff at the Motor Industry Research Association's proving ground, Lindley, Leicestershire.)

MEAN MAXIMUM SPEED: 116 mph (14½-stone rider wearing two-piece trials suit).
HIGHEST ONE-WAY SPEED: 117 mph (still air).
BRAKING: From 30 mph to rest on dry tarmac, 32ft.
TURNING CIRCLE: 13ft 9in.
MINIMUM NON-SNATCH SPEED: 18 mph in top gear.
WEIGHT PER CC: 0.56 lb.

Following pages: carried on Isolastic mountings within a special frame, the Commando engine was descended directly from the 745 cc Atlas (*Don Morley, All-Sport*)

BSA Rocket 3

From an engineering standpoint, the three-cylinder BSA Rocket 3 and its Triumph Trident sister might have been that shade better, had they been designed from the ground up, using a clean sheet of paper. Surely the logical way of splitting a three-cylinder crankcase assembly would have been along the horizontal centre-line? But, instead, the joints were in a vertical plane, with the centre section (incorporating the gearbox shell) flanked by two crankcase halves which came from a vertical twin—the 'Three' was basically a Triumph Tiger 100-and-a-half, with typical Meriden camshafts, timing gear, and valve layout. Even the pushrod tubes, nestling between pairs of cylinders, were standard Triumph design.

Of course it is possible that in the mid-1960s, when work on the new design began, the BSA Group did not have the capital available for a complete retooling operation. But another factor was that this was no pie-in-the-sky project from the Umberslade Hall boffins. The designers were the down-to-earth 'old firm' of Bert Hopwood and Doug Hele, and all the detailing and development—for both the BSA and Triumph versions—was carried out at Triumph's Meriden plant.

A three-cylinder the new unit may have been, but it was so arranged as to make use of the twin-cylinder tooling and techniques that had been tried and proved over a long period.

Basically, the BSA and Triumph Threes were alike, but the Rocket 3 carried its cylinder block at a slight forward inclination, and the frame in which it sat was a duplex cradle design. The Triumph Trident—initially, anyway—had upright cylinders, and a single-front-down-tube frame of Bonneville type.

The demand had come from the USA, for a superbike with a power output of around 60 bhp, with the capability of further development. Bert Hopwood thought that 650 cc was the limit for a vertical twin (beyond that capacity there would be vibration problems), but on the other hand a four-cylinder engine would be wider than was desirable. So that is why a triple was chosen.

The design departed from previous practice by transferring the alternator to the right-hand end of the crankshaft, and by using a car-type diaphragm clutch running on an outrigger bearing for greater rigidity. Primary drive was by triple-row chain.

The most intriguing feature of all was a one-piece crankshaft, a product of the BSA forge at Small Heath which was made, initially, with the three crank throws all lying in the same plane. The steel forging was then reheated and twisted, until the throws were equally spaced at 120 degrees. The first prototype had a

Together with its Triumph Trident sister, the BSA Rocket 3 earned a formidable racing reputation, both in the USA and on home circuits, where Derby rider John Cooper was the star performer

Mike Hailwood leads the 1970 Daytona 200 on a BSA Rocket 3. It was later sidelined by overheating

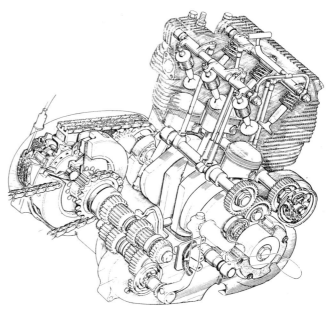

Ghosted view of the Rocket 3 engine-gear unit, showing the one-piece forged crankshaft, triplex primary chain, and Borg and Beck diaphragm clutch. The alternator was housed in the timing chest

cast-iron cylinder block, and was fired by way of a modified six-cylinder car distributor, but in production there was an all-alloy engine, and a contact-breaker unit carried in the timing cover, in which were three sets of points.

The reason for producing two versions of the triple simultaneously was that in the USA the BSA and Triumph distributors were independent bodies, each with its network of sales outlets. Nevertheless, BSA's Small Heath complex was responsible for manufacture of the power units for both makes.

As originally announced, the Rocket 3 and the Trident were reserved for export only, and the first examples did not reach British dealers until April, 1969. Claimed output was 58 bhp at 7,250 rpm, and the speed potential was said to be about 120 mph.

In the USA, the machines proved to be instant successes, and their race capabilities were displayed in the 1970 Daytona 200-mile event—a race which meant very little to the British public, but which had enormous advertising value in its own country. That year, Triumph Tridents finished second and third, but far better things were to follow.

Race-wise, 1971 was the real Year of the Threes. Again the scene was Daytona, with World Road Racing Champion Mike Hailwood spearheading the BSA-Triumph onslaught. Mike took the lead, too, before retiring with mechanical problems. But it was still a day of glory for the Three, with Dick Mann (BSA Rocket 3) the winner at a record 104·7 mph average; a

In its final (mid-1971) guise, the Rocket 3 was greatly influenced by the demands of Californian dealers, hence the vestigial front mud-guard and small fuel tank. Unhappily, BSA tried to sell it in Britain in this form, too

Triumph Trident was second, and another Rocket 3 third.

At home, Ray Pickrell (BSA) won the Thruxton marathon—now a Grand Prix d'Endurance round—and John Cooper beat Giacomo Agostini in the Mallory Park Race of the Year, and in the Brand's Hatch Race of the South, then won the 250-mile event at Ontario, California.

In June, the Isle of Man staged the second production-machine TT, and saw Ray Pickrell and Tony Jefferies finish first and second on Triumph Tridents, with Bob Heath third on a BSA Rocket 3.

Before that, in May, a new and rather jazzed-up version of the Rocket 3 had gone into production, with high-rise handlebar, small tank, humped seat, 'megaphone'-looking silencers, skimpy mudguards and the headlamp hung on bent wire brackets; pretty obviously, the product of Umberslade Hall's frenetic styling department. It was to be the final version of the BSA triple, because July, 1971 saw the closure of the Small Heath competitions shop, and the start of the run-down of BSA as a whole.

Perhaps, if the Threes could have been marketed just a little sooner, things might have been different, but they had only a few months in which to become established on the USA scene before the arrival of a most formidable challenger in the form of the 750 cc Honda 4. It was to the credit of BSA-Triumph that the Trident and Rocket 3 licked the Hondas out of sight in every contest in which they were matched. Yet it has to be conceded that the Honda was more sophisticated in design—or if you prefer it, more gimmicky—and scored in that respect.

Even after the collapse of BSA, and the shotgun marriage which led to the setting up of Norton-Villiers-Triumph, the Triple did not die. It re-emerged as the Triumph T160 Trident, with the refinement of electric starting, but built at Small Heath. And despite the Trident name, the engine was the inclined version which had originally graced the BSA Rocket 3. The model was the last motor cycle to be built in the historic Small Heath factory (the final batch of Threes, all in white, were to police specification and destined to be flown out to Saudi Arabia). The last bike came off the line, in the week before Christmas, 1975—and for old times sake, the 80 workers still there, and due to become redundant that day, gave it temporary BSA instead of Triumph tank badges.

Following pages: not quite to catalogue colour, but handsome for all that, a 741 cc BSA Rocket 3 in a dramatic setting (*Andrew Morland*)

125

740cc BSA ROCKET 3

Racing power with garden-party manners, an iron hand in a velvet glove—such is the dream of many a connoisseur. In the 740 cc Rocket 3, BSA translate the dream into reality. Its 58 bhp is a level of power that any road racer bar those with factory support would give his eye-teeth for.

Motor Cycle road test

Naturally, with just about every mod con you could wish for, the Rocket 3 weighs half as much again as a 500 cc racer. Yet its eager engine provides shattering acceleration and a top whack, with the rider tucked in as much as possible, of more than two miles a minute. And all with no more than a pleasant drone from the six tail pipes.

At the opposite end of the performance scale, the bike will rustle through 30-mph limits in top gear, sounding for all the world like a well-oiled sewing machine.

At both extremes, thanks to the 240-deg firing intervals and the rubber cush-drive in the clutch sprocket, the power is delivered with great silkiness. Moreover, the 120-deg crank spacing gives a degree of engine smoothness, which, while not perfect, is a considerable improvement on parallel-twin standards.

An acceleration graph as steep as the one in this report is a delight to any enthusiast's eye. Sampling that sort of sustained get-up-and-go, in all its seeming effortlessness, is the greatest thrill in the Rocket 3's repertoire.

The magic ton comes up in less than 14 sec. Even with the rider sitting bolt upright at the high-rise handlebar and a pillion passenger behind him, the 105 mph maximum, after a 95-mph change into top gear, is reached in a breathtakingly short time.

Such performance makes a joke of the British 70-mph speed limit. Not only is a top-gear 70 mph sustained on the merest whiff of throttle, but the speed can be regained in a flash after a baulk. (Even from rest, it takes less than 10 sec).

It is possible to visualise conditions of wind and gradient that would prevent the Rocket 3 from holding 70 mph. That speed is not only far below the third-gear maximum, it can be reached also in second without exceeding the safe maximum of 8,000 rpm.

Indeed, the snap acceleration was found to be as great a safety factor as the smooth, powerful braking.

For normal riding, the engine is not oversensitive to rpm. With some 6 cwt of metal and muscle to shift, its smooth, low-speed torque gets you off the mark like a gentle giant, and the clutch is home within a couple of yards.

But if you are a glutton for the heftiest and most prolonged kick in the pants, then it pays to keep the revs above 4,500 to 5,000 rpm. What vibration there is starts to make itself felt at about 5,000 rpm, peaks at 5,500 to 6,000 rpm, then dies down again.

Five-star performance, in the case of the Rocket 3, demands five-star fuel if the

As Vic Willoughby finds above, riding position is relaxed and cornering effortless in spite of the Rocket 3's weight

engine is not to pink when the twistgrip is tweaked at lowish revs.

In the mid-speed range, the engine has quite a modest thirst. Riding at the legal limits on long trips gave 50 mpg in spite of plenty of hard acceleration. It was only in full-speed tests at the MIRA proving ground that the figure dropped to some 40 mpg.

Cold starting was a first-kick affair and not a very lusty kick at that. The only

prior drill necessary was to close the air lever and lightly flood the outside carburettors (the middle tickler is hard to get at).

Brisk prod

For hot starting, however, throttle position was found to be critical and the

Tucked unobtrusively between side covers beneath the fuel tank is the oil cooler in the scavenge line

twistgrip had to be set precisely as for a fast tickover before giving the starter a brisk prod.

While the engine would idle as slowly as 500 rpm, it was found best to set the throttle stop for 800 rpm if all risk of stalling was to be avoided. Some valve-gear clatter was noticeable when the machine was stationary, though not when on the move.

Firm and inclined to be heavy to operate, the clutch was smooth, free from drag and complete master of the engine's high torque. Bottom-gear engagement at rest was noiseless and neutral indexing

was very positive, whether from bottom or second gear.

The gear change was stiffer to operate than on most machines, though, and a bit clonky when going up. Slick downward changes were helped by the speed of the engine's response to a tiny blip of the twistgrip.

On first acquaintance, the Rocket 3 seems very high and wide in the seat, especially for small riders. In no time at all, however, you feel at home in the densest traffic; for the bike is one of those

Rider's-eye view shows the instrument panel with ammeter and oil-pressure and main-beam lights separating the 150-mph speedometer and 10,000-rpm revmeter. Petrol filler cap has a quick-release, snap-down action

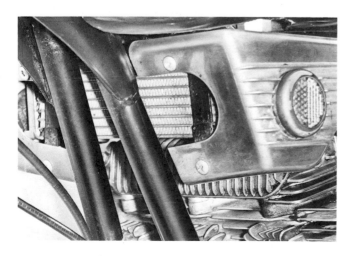

that can be ridden to a standstill feet-up, with no conscious steering correction, and there is no feeling of top-heaviness when stretching a toe to the ground.

Riders of all sizes found the relationship of footrests, seat and handlebar extremely comfortable for normal riding. Only when holding top speed for miles on end was there an impression of stopping as much air as a barn door. In those circumstances, using the rear footrests brought some relief from the need to hang on. Most British riders would probably specify the lower handlebar.

The pillion position is equally comfortable, while the dualseat is generous in size, luxuriously padded and raised at the rear.

No designer welcomes weight but, suspensionwise, it does have the advantage of increasing the ratio of sprung to unsprung weight. That factor, and the effective damping of the Girling rear struts and the front-fork shuttle valves, make for excellent roadholding with neither pitching nor harshness.

The Rocket 3 is very surefooted. Flip-flop cornering, at speeds up to about 80 mph, calls for relatively light pressure from the outside knee. Indeed, it was a great delight to swirl through twisty lanes, blending throttle action with banking—and with no furniture scraping the ground.

Naturally, though, when you are boring into a self-made gale, bumpy bends call for a firm effort with the arms as well as the legs. But at no time was the steering damper brought into use.

The combination of weight and speed demands first-class braking—and this the Rocket 3 has. Press the controls at full speed and the bike dips its nose purposefully as the shoes bite. Yet so smooth and progressive is the action that there are no qualms from that score in the wet.

The lighting, too, is well up to scratch; but the windtone horns, though giving a note entirely in keeping with the bike's aristocratic bearing, need a lot more power.

Although it operates three carbs, the twistgrip is delightfully light and sweet in action. All controls are well placed, though you have to reach forward under the handlebar to get at the three-position tumbler switch for the lights.

Both prop and centre stands are robust and well up to their work. Since it has no extension-piece, however, the prop is inaccessible and is difficult to bring out with the toe of one's boot. Putting the bike on the centre stand entails a fair degree of effort but the lifting rail is well placed and a simultaneous thrust on the stand's foot-piece helps.

For the sheer fun of it, the Rocket 3 was given a hard caning on test. Yet it finished

Secured by three coin-slot fasteners, the main left-side cover is removed for access to the battery, tool compartment and air filter

with little of its engine oil outside and only the slightest spattering on the left side of the rear-wheel rim.

Without question, the Rocket 3 is one of the most exciting machines ever to come off a production line. It cannot help but delight not only the Statesiders who demanded it in the first place but any rider with a generous share of red blood—plus the experience and judgement to back it up.

specification

ENGINE: Capacity and type: 740 cc (67 x 70mm) overhead-valve transverse three. Bearings: ball driving side, roller timing side and two plain inner mains; plain big-ends. Lubrication: dry sump, capacity 5½ pints; oil cooler. Compression ratio: 9 to 1. Carburettors: three Amal 626 Concentrics with 27mm-diameter chokes; air slides operated by handlebar lever; felt-and-mesh air filter. Claimed output, 58 bhp at 7,250 rpm.
TRANSMISSION: Primary: ⅜in triplex chain in oilbath case with adjustable, rubber-faced, spring-blade tensioner. Secondary: ⅝ x ⅜in chain. Clutch: dry single-plate Borg and Beck with diaphragm spring. Gear ratios: 11.95, 8.3, 5.83 to 4.87 to 1. Engine rpm at 30 mph in top gear: 1,950.
ELECTRICAL EQUIPMENT: Ignition: battery and three Siba coils. Charging: Lucas 110-watt RM20 alternator through rectifier and diode to 12-volt, 8-amp-hour battery. Headlamp: Lucas 7in-diameter, flat-back type with 50/40-watt main bulb.
FUEL CAPACITY: 4½ gallons.
TYRES: Dunlop 3.25 x 19in ribbed front, 4.10 x 19in K81 rear.
BRAKES: 8in-diameter, twin-leading-shoe front; 7in-diameter, single leading-shoe rear; finger adjusters.
SUSPENSION: Telescopic front fork with two-way hydraulic damping; pivoted rear fork controlled by Girling spring-and-hydraulic struts with three-position adjustment for load.
DIMENSIONS: Wheelbase, 58in; ground clearance, 6½in; seat height, 32in. All unladen.
WEIGHT: 488 lb, including one gallon of fuel.
PRICE: To be announced.
ROAD TAX: £10 a year; £3 13s for four months.
MAKERS: BSA Motor Cycles Ltd, Armoury Road, Birmingham 11.

performance

(Obtained by "Motor Cycle" staff at the Motor Industry Research Association's Proving Ground, Lindley Leicestershire.)
MEAN MAXIMUM SPEED: 122 mph (10½-stone rider wearing racing leathers)
HIGHEST ONE-WAY SPEED: 122 mph (still air).
BRAKING: From 30 mph to rest on dry tarmac, 32ft 6in.
TURNING CIRCLE: 15ft 5in.
MINIMUM NON-SNATCH SPEED: 23 mph in top gear.
WEIGHT PER CC: 0.66 lb.

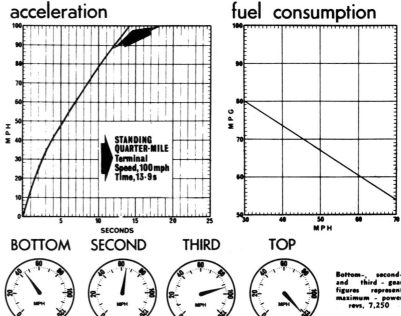

acceleration

STANDING QUARTER-MILE Terminal Speed, 100 mph Time, 13·9s

fuel consumption

BOTTOM SECOND THIRD TOP

Bottom-, second- and third - gear figures represent maximum - power revs, 7,250

Triumph T100T Daytona

There are two excellent reasons for bringing the vivacious Triumph Daytona into a collection of classics of the 1960s. First, it gives a sight of a Triumph C-range model—the 350 and 500 cc machines which introduced unit construction to the twins of the Meriden range. And second, the name reflects what was probably the most glorious racing performance by British machinery on foreign soil in recent years—the 1966 and 1967 wins by Meriden-prepared 490 cc Triumphs (handled by American riders) in the prestigious Daytona 200 races.

The first C-range twin to appear was the 348 cc 3TA Twenty-One, announced in February of 1957. This was an unusual model name, chosen because it was, in American parlance, a 21 cubic inch job, and it celebrated the 21st anniversary of the take-over by the new Triumph Engineering Company Ltd, of the motor-cycle side of the original Triumph Company.

In the 3TA (and, a little later, its 490 cc 5TA Speed Twin sister) Triumph tried to preach the gospel of rear wheel enclosure. Triumph advertising of the time proclaimed it as, 'The machine with a wheel in tomorrow'. But not every rider appreciated such trendiness, and the rear enclosure—derided as the 'bathtub'—was stripped off and discarded, as often as not. Ironically, present-day restorers, hoping to put 3TA and 5TA models back to catalogue condition, are currently seeking such discarded bathtubs, and are even talking of having replica tinware made, in glassfibre . . .

That, however, is introductory, and from the soft-tuned Twenty-One and Speed Twin were later derived a couple of rather more lively models, the three-fifty taking the name of Tiger 90, while the 490 cc version revived the famous Tiger 100 title.

At the behest of Triumph's USA subsidiary, Doug Hele and his merry men of the Meriden competitions department set to work in 1966 to produce a batch of very special machines, based on the Tiger 100, specifically for the Daytona race meeting. Works tester Percy Tait had already been racing a developed Tiger 100 on the home short circuits, and experience gained with this model was ploughed back into the machines for Daytona.

The Tiger 100 origin was obvious, but now there was a cylinder head carrying twin $1\frac{3}{16}$-in choke Amal Grand Prix carburettors on parallel inlet tracts. The inlet ports were opened out to suit, of course, cam profiles were akin to those of a Bonneville six-fifty, and the Elektron timing cover carried an outboard contact-breaker unit running on independent bearings and, therefore less subject to any fluctuation in the points gap.

Crankcase ventilation was revised, and the crankcase was now vented into the primary chaincase, from which a large-bore plastic pipe carried the waste gases to the tail of the rear mudguard. To keep the oil temperature as constant as may be in the arduous conditions envisaged, a small oil cooler was mounted at the right-hand front of the engine.

What happened is history. Buddy Elmore took his Triumph to a record race average speed of 96·58 mph, crossing the line

The Triumph works 500 cc racer, built for the 1966 Daytona event. The blister on the timing cover hides a special contact-breaker unit running on an independent bearing

ahead of two works-entered 750 cc Harley-Davidsons.

Triumphs had been considering marketing a super-sports, twin-carburettor edition of the Tiger 100, anyway, and this brilliant victory gave them the impetus. The name of the new model was ready-made—the Daytona, naturally. Like the racers, it boasted twin carburettors, although these were Amal Monoblocs (each with its own air cleaner) instead of the pukka Grand Prix instruments. But it did have bigger inlet valves, Bonneville cams, a 9 to 1 compression ratio, and a most respectable power output of 39 bhp.

This, then, was the production 490 cc T100T Daytona, new for the 1967 season and introducing a new frame with a reduced steering-head angle, and a more robust construction around the rear fork pivot. This frame was transferred to the 348 cc Tiger 90, and single-carburettor 490 cc Tiger 100, also; but with the coming of the Daytona, the more docile 3TA and 5TA models were dropped—and with the departure of the 5TA the traditional Speed Twin name, which had marked Edward Turner's first Triumph twin in 1937, had gone for good.

With one Daytona success under their belts, the Triumph folk had tasted blood, and so the winter of 1966-7 saw a further batch of six models being tended by Doug Hele and company at Meriden, in readiness for the March meeting. Mechanically, they were little different to the 1966 models, but the front fork was shorter, and the bike sat on 18-in instead of 19-in wheels, so making a much lower profile. There was also a slimmer, flat-sided fuel tank, as used on the machine campaigned by Percy Tait on the home tracks, and a more aerodynamic fairing.

With Doug Hele as pit manager, Triumph looked all set for a repeat victory. And they got it! The early leader had been Dick Hammer, but Dick slid off, remounting and rejoining the race. In the later stages, Gary Nixon, and 1966 winner Buddy Elmore, held a secure first and second, and so the six works Triumphs came home—in 1st, 2nd, 7th, 8th, 9th and 15th positions. Nixon had blasted round to set a new lap record of 98·23 mph, and such was the pace that only he and Elmore were on the same lap at the finish.

It has to be said that the following year, Harley-Davidsons gained revenge, while in later Daytona meetings the Triumph effort was concentrated on the three-cylinder Tridents. But the little Daytona twin had had its hours of glory. Nor must it be forgotten that Daytonas would give a good account of themselves in the Isle of Man production-machine races run from 1967 onward, and that Daytona power units would be employed by Britain's International Six Days men (albeit in Cheney frames).

For the 1969 season there would be further improvements to

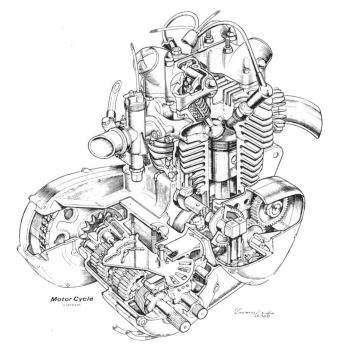

Motor Cyclé

All Triumph unit-construction 350 and 500 cc twins were derived from this 1957 3TA Twenty-One, the name celebrating the firm's 21st anniversary. The Daytona twin had twin carburettors and a timing-chest-mounted contact breaker unit

the road-going Daytona, which was to benefit from racing experience by acquiring a redesigned crankshaft layout, with ball-bearing instead of plain timing-side main, and an axial oil feed into the crankshaft core and thence to the big-ends. An 8-in twin-leading-shoe front brake, and an oil warning light operated by a pressure switch were further embellishments. By that time, though, the 348 cc Tiger 90 had been dropped, and in a shortened list of models only the Tiger 100 and Daytona remained of the one-time C-range twins.

Apart from a change of colour, from bright green to claret-and-silver, the Daytona was to live out the few years that remained to it with no further modification. A casualty of the Meriden workers' sit-in, it failed to return to the range when the factory restarted production under co-operative ownership. But it is a model worth remembering, for all that. Big is not always beautiful, and certainly the Daytona which the author owned for five years gave faithful, always-willing service with no call for major overhaul.

This battle between Percy Tait (81, Triumph) and Dave Croxford (80, Matchless) enlivened the May, 1967, Castle Combe races. Croxford won, with Tait second. Race experience such as this was built into the production Triumph Daytona sports mount

490cc TRIUMPH T100T DAYTONA

Our tastes are often fickle. Way back the five-hundred twin reigned supreme in the larger-capacity Then the demand was for bigger cylinders and the six-fifty became more popular; now the seven-fifty is on the up-and-up.

Motor Cycle road test

Yet many owners would find that a top-rate five-hundred, such as the Triumph Daytona, a super-sports roadster with twin carburettors, would provide all the performance they can use. In addition it would offer advantages of saving in purchase price and running costs, and in handling.

With a mean top speed of 104 mph and a very presentable acceleration curve, the Daytona can put out averages on give-and-take roads that are up with the best six-fifties. Slightly different riding techniques are required, of course. The bigger bikes provide more bottom-end power whereas an engine such as the Daytona needs high revs to give of its best, and this means frequent gear changing.

Below 3,000 rpm power is only moderate. As the revs build up towards 4,000 so does the power, and at 6,000 the horses are being punched out. From there to peak at 8,000 rpm, the power continues its upward surge, though, in practice, it was found unnecessary to let the revs go higher than about 7,000 before changing gear.

Gearing is lowish and the ratios closely spaced to provide optimum acceleration. This is sensible policy since Britain's overall 70-mph limit makes flashing acce-

Hard to guess that the twin-carburettor engine started life as a 70-mph three-fifty almost a dozen years ago

leration far more useful than high maximum speed.

From a standstill, best results are obtained by slipping the clutch in the initial few yards to get the engine buzzing into the useful power band, and from 4,000 rpm the bike is really on its way.

In the unrestricted acres of the MIRA proving ground, the Daytona provided an effortless 80-mph cruising gait, with ample power reserve to exceed 90 mph—and there was no need for the rider to tuck in.

Though the handlebar is rubber-mounted, some high-frequency vibration was felt at about 4,500 rpm. It increased as the revs went higher, though it could not be called excessive or above average for good parallel twins.

Starting

Before the first start of the day, the clutch required unsticking by sharply depressing the pedal with the handlebar lever raised. Starting demanded no more than closing

On a sunny day in the Isle of Man, David Dixon bend-swinging the sporty Daytona

of the air lever, lightly flooding both carburettors—they are matched, with ticklers outward and thus easily accessible—and a swing on the kickstarter. With a cold or hot engine, one prod usually did the trick.

From cold, the air control could be gradually opened within the first quarter-mile.

Idling varied from a fairly reliable 1,400 rpm to an inconsistent 1,000 rpm, and there was tendency to stalling on stopping at, say, traffic lights. No air leaks could be located and the fault could not be remedied by carburettor adjustments.

Clatter

Mechanical clatter came chiefly from the valve gear, though it was noticeable only when stationary and at low speeds.

The riding position is a good compro-

Following pages: last survivor of Triumph's 500 cc twins was the T100T Daytona, seen here in 1968 trim (*National Motorcycle Museum*)

mise for riders of widely varying build. Layout of the footrests, handlebar and seat provides a slight forward lean to combat air pressure yet is comfortable at town speeds, while the rear of the fuel tank is sensibly narrow for knee grip. Positioning of hand and foot controls is ideal, but the twistgrip was slightly heavy in operation although it was well greased and the cable thoroughly oiled.

Wide, well-padded and with cross-ribs to prevent the rider from sliding around, the seat was a boon and proved completely comfortable on day trips in excess of 350 miles.

Manoeuvrability is a big point in the Daytona's favour. Feeling no heavier than some two-fifties, it could be ridden zestfully yet safely.

No grounding

Light and sensitive, steering was reassuringly positive on fast, main-road bends and the steering damper seemed quite

Latest mounting for the capacitors is in a rubber housing beneath the nose of the fuel tank. Note the rubber mounting for the tank

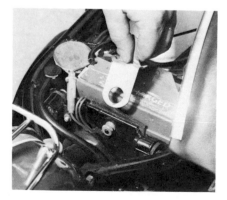

The Lucas battery is retained in place by a rubber strap, the metal tongue of which is located in a grooved nut on the carrier. The battery itself is mounted in rubber to isolate it from vibration

performance

(Obtained by "Motor Cycle" staff at the Motor Industry Research Association's Proving Ground, Lindley, Leicestershire.)
MEAN MAXIMUM SPEED: 104 mph (13-stone rider wearing one-piece racing leathers)
HIGHEST ONE-WAY SPEED: 107 mph (moderate following wind)
BRAKING: From 30 mph to rest on dry tarmac, 28ft 6in.
TURNING CIRCLE: 18ft 3in.
MINIMUM NON-SNATCH SPEED: 23 mph in top gear.
WEIGHT PER CC: 0.72 lb.

specification

ENGINE: Capacity and type, 490 cc (69 x 65.5mm) overhead-valve twin. Bearings: two ball-journal mains, plain big ends. Lubrication: dry sump, capacity 6 pints. Compression ratio 9.7 to 1. Carburettors: Amal 626 Concentrics with felt-and-mesh air filters, air slides operated by handlebar lever. Claimed output, 39 bhp at 8,000 rpm
TRANSMISSION: Primary, ⅜in duplex chain in oilbath case. Secondary ⅝ x ⅜in chain. Clutch multi-plate. Gear ratios 14.1, 9.2, 6.9 and 5.7 to 1. Engine rpm at 30 mph in top gear, 2,300
ELECTRICAL EQUIPMENT: Ignition battery and twin coils. Charging Lucas 110-watt alternator through rectifier and diode to 12-volt, 8-amphour battery. Headlamp: Lucas 7in-diameter, with 50/40-watt main bulb
FUEL CAPACITY: 3 gallons, reserve supply
TYRES: Avon 3.25 x 18in ribbed front, 3.50 x 18in studded rear.
BRAKES: 8in-diameter front and 7in-diameter rear, with floating shoes; finger adjusters.
SUSPENSION: Triumph telescopic front fork with hydraulic damping;

Twin Amal Concentric carburettors replace the Monoblocs formerly used and the 8-in diameter front brake is a worthwhile improvement. Traditional and useful feature is the tank-top grille

pivoted rear fork controlled by Girling spring-and-hydraulic units with three-position adjustment for load.
DIMENSIONS: Wheelbase, 53½in; ground clearance, 7⅛in; seat height, 30in. All unladen.
WEIGHT: 356 lb, including one gallon of petrol.
PRICE: £345 16s 8d. Extras on test machine: revmeter, £9 9s 10; quickly detachable rear wheel, £5 9s 3d; pillion footrests, £1 9s; prop stand, £1 10s 3d; steering lock, 19s 10
ROAD TAX: £10 a year, £3 13s for four months
MAKERS: Triumph Engineering Co Ltd, Meriden Works, Allesley, Coventry

The diode is now in a neat torpedo-shape casting and is placed well out in the air stream, directly beneath the headlamp. The diode is positively earthed to the frame by separate wiring, not through the mounting bracket

acceleration

STANDING
QUARTER-MILE
Terminal
Speed, 88 mph
Time, 15·5 s

fuel consumption

BOTTOM   SECOND   THIRD   TOP

Bottom-, second-
and third-gear
figures represent
maximum-power
revs, 8,000

superfluous. Noticeable lack of top hamper encouraged slick cornering and the bike could be leaned well over without fear of anything grounding.

Much of the test mileage was on wet roads, so the Daytona had ample opportunity to show any vices—it had none.

Both front and rear suspensions are on the firm side. The well-damped front fork is an excellent example of its type; it worked smoothly on all surfaces and without any suggestion of clashing even on the sharpest of bumps.

Though set at the minimum pre-load, the rear units failed to iron out major road shocks and for riders of average weight the comfort level would be improved by lower-poundage springs.

Both brakes performed well. Light in operation, they provided powerful retardation from top speeds yet remained ideally controllable for use when riding on wet, city streets. When applied fiercely in crash stops at MIRA, their power was outstanding; the front brake squealed the tyre on the emery-like surface without locking the wheel. During prolonged riding on rain-soaked roads, neither brake suffered from water on the linings.

Main-beam lighting was good enough to allow daytime speeds after dark and the dip-beam prevented dazzle. A worthwhile detail is the use of a three-position toggle switch on top of the headlamp shell; it proved easier to operate than rotary-type switches. The horn note was totally inadequate for the performance of the machine.

Lubrication of the rear chain is set by means of a valve inside the oil-tank filler neck. After adjustment, the system worked well. In normal use the chain required resetting at 500-mile intervals.

A good quality tool roll is provided and was found to be adequate for routine maintenance.

Finished in green and matt-silver, with the usual parts chromium-plated, the Daytona is what it looks—a highly-developed, purposeful, practical sportster for the enthusiast.

Both Concentric carburettors have large-capacity, felt-and-mesh air filters. Removable plate at the front of the primary chaincase is for checking the ignition timing by strobe

Neat and compact, the Daytona has no frills

Velocette Venom Thruxton

The ploy of a manufacturer naming his top sports model after a well-known race venue is of many years' standing. Triumph, and several other makers, listed a 'TT Model' before the First World War; Norton had a Brooklands Special in 1920; Rudge produced the Ulster; and coming to more recent times, there have been the Ducati Monza, and Moto Guzzi Le Mans.

Such names do lend a bike a certain cachet, particularly if there is justification for their use. In the post-war years, the Southampton Club's production-machine marathon at Thruxton airfield (at first called the Nine-Hour, but later the 500-Mile) attracted a great deal of interest among the public at large. Not that they actually went to *watch* the event which, let's face it, became terribly confusing for the onlooker after the first few laps. But they were tremendously interested in the results because these, after all, were achieved on bikes basically the same as those they rode every day, modified for racing within certain limitations.

One make which distinguished itself in Thruxton 500-Mile events of the 1950s was Velocette, usually with 500 cc Venom singles entered by enthusiastic dealers such as Geoff Dodkin. And it was through race experience gained in this way that, in October 1964, a high-performance race kit for the Venom was offered by the factory.

The kit comprised an entirely new cylinder head, with a narrower valve angle, an inlet valve increased to 2 in diameter, and an inlet tract altered to give greater swirl angle to the ingoing gas. Mounted at a steep downdraught angle was a $1\frac{3}{8}$-in choke Amal Grand Prix carburettor, the fitting of which necessitated new oil and fuel tanks, cut away to clear the carburettor intake bellmouth.

So far, so good, but within a year the prototype of a complete super-sports Venom incorporating the race kit and also featuring clip-on racing handlebars, a humpy-back racing seat, rear-set footrests and controls, and twin-leading-shoe front brake, was on the road. This, then, was the Venom Thruxton, and David Dixon gave it a thorough try-out for *The Motor Cycle*, by riding it, in pouring rain, down to Castle Combe circuit, then across to Mallory Park, and finally down to Silverstone, squirting it around each track for several flat-out laps.

It was, he reported, quick yet perfectly tractable for road use, and he was able to cruise between circuits at 90 mph-plus (there was no blanket 70 mph speed limit in those days, remember?).

The 499 cc Velocette Venom Thruxton on which Jean-Louis Renaud gained the 1967 French National 500 cc Championship

At the end of 1965, the machine entered the Velocette catalogue as the 499 cc Venom Thruxton, priced at £369 19s 2d (£369·96), and graced with a most handsome silver tank with blue lining. Even better, instead of the modern plastic badgery of the more humdrum Velocette models, this one had the hallowed name carried by traditional-style gold transfers. Decals, if you must have it in American.

Yet Velocette missed the boat, just slightly. Here was the brand-new Thruxton sportster. But the same year, the Southampton Club had abandoned Thruxton as a venue, and moved the 500-miler for 1965 to Castle Combe, in Wiltshire. Not that it mattered much, for Velocette machines again made all the running in the 500 cc class of the event.

Initially the model shared by Howard German and Chris Williams led, until a snapped connecting rod put paid to their efforts. Then the Ellis Boyce and Tom Phillips machine took over, only to drop out with lack of compression, while leading the 500 cc pack at half-distance. So in the end yet another Velocette, ridden by Joe Dunphy and David Dixon, got the chequered flag, despite having lost time earlier on with water in the magneto.

In time, the Thruxton-type front fork and twin-leading-shoe front brake were adopted as standard on the Viper and Venom Clubman models, too, so gaining them Mk. II rating. As a result of a strong demand from traditionalist customers, the Venom Thruxton was offered from 1967 on with the alternative of a black tank with gold lining and name transfer, instead of silver and blue lining.

That year (1967) the 500-Mile marathon had moved yet again, this time to Brands Hatch. Once again a Geoff Dodkin tuned and entered Velocette Venom Thruxton was prime favourite for 500 cc honours, with Reg Everett and Tom Phillips sharing the riding. For hour after hour the machine ran like a train, and with only an hour to run before the finish flag went out, it was leading its class by an astounding eight clear laps; moreover, it was lying third in the overall classification, among big Triumphs and Nortons.

But chickens must never be counted before eggs are hatched, and at just about that point the Velo went silent—the mag had packed up again. Even so, it was possible to wait just short of the finishing line, then push it past the flag to claim fourth place in the class, astern of three Triumph Tiger 100s.

Still, there was far better luck in the Isle of Man, where the first-ever Production-machine TT was held. Here the 500 cc-

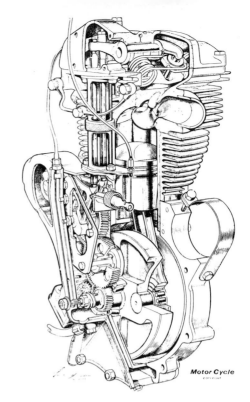

The Velocette 499 cc Venom engine from which the Thruxton 500 unit was developed. Main bearings are of taper-roller type, timing gears have fine-pitch helical teeth, valves are pushrod operated and closed by hairpin springs

class winner was local rider Neil Kelly, at a most respectable average speed of 89·89 mph. In addition, Keith Heckles on another Velo Thruxton came home second at 89·15 mph, the two being well clear of the rest of the field.

Well, at least magneto failure would be a bogey for not much longer, for Lucas, the sole remaining British makers of such an instrument, announced that they were phasing out magneto production. From July, 1968, therefore, all Velocette models went over to battery-and-coil ignition, although the firm stuck to the prehistoric belt-driven 6-volt direct-current dynamo (albeit a Lucas instead of the former Miller).

The trouble was that the narrow Velocette crankcases precluded the fitting of a crankshaft-mounted alternator, unless the stator had been outboard of the engine sprocket. A compromise system, with an alternator housed in the dynamo position and driven by vee-belt, was taken through the development stages and, had the company survived, would have gone into production.

Unfortunately Velocette, a family concern, had invested too heavily in tooling-up for the 249 cc flat-twin two-stroke Viceroy scooter. The Viceroy was a total flop, and a late use of its power unit for propelling a small hovercraft failed to ward off tragedy.

By 1969, when the following road test was carried out, there was very little left in the kitty. That explains why we had to use a second-hand machine—a Venom brought up to 1969 Thruxton specification at the factory—instead of a new bike. New Velocettes were being built in penny numbers only, against firm money-first orders from customers, and no way was there anything to spare with which to build a press road-test model.

The company did manage to survive (just about) through 1970, but that was the end, save for some dealer-assembled models using engines made by the current owner of the Velocette trade-mark, Matt Holder. Second-hand or not, this was to be, sadly, the last press road-test of a Hall Green Velocette.

M. Vasselin, 1966 French 500 cc production-machine champion seen on his Velocette Thruxton at Montlhery Autodrome

499cc VELOCETTE VENOM THRUXTON

If you have spotted the D registration suffix you will know that the bike pictured on this page is a 1966 job. The fact is, it was. Unlike most road-test models, the Thruxton of this story is not factory-supplied but, instead, is privately owned by *Motor Cycle* advertising man in the Midlands, Howard Middleton.

Motor Cycle ROAD IMPRESSION

Readers have been clamouring for a full-scale test of a Velocette Thruxton and we would have been only too happy to oblige long ago—however, the model is still in short supply and the factory have never been able to spare one for test purposes.

So an alternative plot was hatched. Howard had his 1966 bike and the works cooperated by converting it into a 1969 model. It was completely revamped—stripped and rebuilt to the current specification.

The single-cylinder Velocette hasn't changed so very much over the years. In one form or another it has been a familiar sight since the 1930s, but it should not be shrugged off as obsolete or out-dated.

Internal developments, mainly concentrated on cylinder-head tracts and valve diameters, have kept it well abreast of the times. And, certainly, a machine with a 90-mph-plus lap of the Isle of Man course to its credit deserves healthy respect. This lap was put in by Neil Kelly when he won the 500 cc class of the Production TT at an average speed of 89·89 mph two years ago.

Derived from the 499 cc Venom, itself no mean performer, the Thruxton is, in essence, a road-going racer. Equipment includes a special cylinder head with 2-in diameter inlet valve, an Amal GP carburettor, close-ratio gearing, twin-leading-shoe front brake, light-alloy wheel rims, rear-set footrests and controls, and clip-on handle-bars. Take off the lighting equipment, and it is near-enough ready for the starting grid.

Traditionalists to a man, Velo fans were dismayed when, a few months ago, the factory abandoned the hallowed magneto and, in its place, installed direct-current coil ignition; yes, even on the Thruxton.

It was an enforced choice, following a stop to magneto manufacture by Lucas, yet it must be admitted that, as a result, the Thruxton has become much more civilised.

Gentle easing

Formerly, starting was an acquired art, the secrets of which were passed down

The riding position pinpoints the Thruxton's role as a house-trained racer. Note the light-alloy rims, Amal GP carburettor and the heat-shield on the oil tank

from Velo-owning father to son. Now, it is a first- or second-kick exercise calling for nothing more in pre-kick drill than a flooded float-chamber and a gentle easing over compression with the valve-lifter raised.

The distributor unit incorporates an auto-advance mechanism, so it is no longer necessary to juggle with an ignition lever to produce jerk-free running at low rpm.

Bottom-gear ratio, at 10 to 1, is high, and with such an ultra-sporting specification the Thruxton might seem unsuitable for general pottering around. And how about when conditions are really diabolical?

All right, here's the answer. This particular Thruxton, ridden solo, was used by Middleton for the 1969 Dragon Rally and back, plodding along through deep snow at 15 to 20 mph in bottom gear without missing a beat.

Many times on that trip the coil ignition showed its worth, keeping the engine pulling strongly and happily from as low as 1,500 rpm.

Of course, clip-on bars and rear-set rests hardly add up to rider comfort on snowbound roads, but they do come into their own when faster motoring is possible. The semi-racing crouch defeats wind pressure without placing too great a strain on the wrists and arms. The Velo is, above all, an enthusiast's machine and, given an experienced rider, can outperform most other models on the road, six-fifties not excepted.

Superior

The make has long been famed for roadholding, but with its two-way damped front fork the Thruxton is superior even to the Venom. It can be cranked over safely until the footrest ends touch down, and that is way beyond the limits of lean found in normal riding. Ambitious cornering is one of the pleasures of conducting a Thruxton, and the riding position is tailored to suit.

The legal 70-mph limit can be held indefinitely, the engine turning over lazily at a mere 4,000 rpm. Use the gears intelligently, keep the revs above 3,000 and really high averages become possible.

Given freedom from speed limits, as at

For high-speed cruising, the low-set grips and rear-set footrests are ideal

the MIRA circuit, and the bike cruises comfortably in the nineties. Top whack? Our two-way 104 mph figure was recorded on an exceptionally windy day, and though an exhilarating 114 mph was clocked when running with the breeze, the opposite-direction run came down with a bump to just under 95 mph.

In theory, maybe the gain in one way should be compensated by the loss in the other, but this never works out in practice. Under calmer conditions, therefore, the two-way speed could well have been a couple of miles an hour higher.

To match that kind of performance, good brakes are a necessity. The Thruxton brakes were first-class with, in particular, the twin-leading-shoe front unit offering plenty of feel and a reassuring freedom from fade.

Because of the unorthodox design of the Velocette clutch, the uninitiated tend to regard it with suspicion. However, it proved light to operate and coped entirely satisfactorily with everyday usage.

Following pages: Velocette's 500 cc Venom Thruxton, a sportster with a production-racing heritage (*Andrew Morland*)

High gear

Understandably, obtaining of maximum-acceleration figures does give any clutch a caning — especially when, with a high bottom gear, it has to be slipped a lot on the getaway. With this sort of treatment, a strong smell of overheated linings arose after the first few runs, and a brief cooling-off period was allowed before continuing.

Big surprise of the test was the meagre fuel consumption. Viewing the big-bore, racing-style carburettor, a relatively high consumption had been anticipated, but the recorded 96 mpg at a steady 30 mph would have done credit to a touring two-fifty.

It is on the lighting side that the Thruxton falls from grace. To be brutally frank, a six-volt, 60-watt dc system is nowhere near good enough for a machine of this potential. The horn? No better, but no worse, than the average British motor-cycle horn.

On the credit side, the coil ignition set-up is well thought out and the distributor slips very neatly into the former magneto location. Slightly less happy is the siting of the ignition switch at the front of the tool-box lid where the key can chafe against the rider's leg.

Except for a slight leak from the primary chaincase, engine and gearbox remained oiltight. Mechanical noise was low, the muted rustle of the valve gear being lost on the wind at anything above very low speeds.

Characteristically Velocette, the deep chuff-chuff from the lozenge-shape silen-

cer fell pleasantly on the ear; an old-fashioned sound, recalling a more spacious age, but totally inoffensive.

If there seemed to be more carburettor intake roar than usual, the reason was plain enough—more carburettor than usual and no air filter.

Some vibration could be felt, but it was of a low-frequency nature, not at all off-putting to the rider and soon forgotten. It disappeared at 4,500 rpm, to return at above the 6,200 rpm line, but this was, in any case, over-revving the engine.

Routine maintenance produced no problems but one minor annoyance, in that the silencer has to be detached before

All Velocette four-stroke singles employed a front-mounted dynamo driven by belt from a pulley on the engine shaft

the rear wheel can be extracted.

A real flyer of a model, the Velocette Thruxton has a long record of production-race successes. Without doubt, that list will grow longer. To condemn it to a life among city streets would be sheer cruelty to machinery, but owner Howard Middleton is a long-distance rally addict, and for fun of that nature the Thruxton must come very close indeed to the ideal mount.

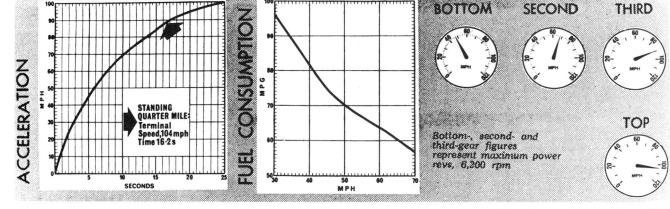

ACCELERATION

STANDING QUARTER MILE: Terminal Speed,104 mph Time 16·2 s

FUEL CONSUMPTION

BOTTOM   SECOND   THIRD

Bottom-, second- and third-gear figures represent maximum power revs, 6,200 rpm

TOP

SPECIFICATION

ENGINE: Capacity and type: 499 cc (86 x 86mm) overhead-valve single. Bearings: two taper-roller mains, caged roller big end. Lubrication: dry sump, oil-tank capacity, 4 pints. Compression ratio: 9 to 1. Carburettor: Amal 5GP2, 1⅜in-choke, with remote float chamber; air slide operated from handlebar; no air filter. Claimed output: 41 bhp at 6,200 rpm.

TRANSMISSION: Primary, ⅜ x 0.305in chain, in oilbath; secondary, ⅝ x ⅜in

chain. Clutch: multiplate. Gear ratios: 10.1, 6.97, 5.3 and 4.4 to 1. Engine rpm at 30 mph in top gear, 1,550.

ELECTRICAL EQUIPMENT: Battery and coil. Charging: Lucas 60-watt dc dynamo to six-volt, 13-amp-hour battery through automatic voltage control unit. Headlamp: Lucas 7in-diameter with 30/24-watt main bulb.

FUEL CAPACITY: 4¼ gallons.

BRAKES: 7½in-diameter 2LS front; 7in-diameter rear, finger adjuster on rear.

TYRES: Dunlop 19 x 3.00in ribbed front; 19 x 3.50in studded rear.

SUSPENSION: Telescopic front fork with two-way hydraulic damping.

Pivoted rear fork controlled by Girling spring-and-hydraulic units with three-position adjustment for load; additional load adjustment by varying angle of inclination.

DIMENSIONS: Wheelbase, 53⅜in; ground clearance, 5½in; seat height, 30½in; all unladen.

WEIGHT: 390 lb, including approximately one gallon of petrol.

PRICE: £400 1s 10d, including British purchase tax.

ROAD TAX: £10 a year; £3 13s for four months.

MANUFACTURERS: Veloce Ltd, York Road, Hall Green, Birmingham, 28.

PERFORMANCE

(Obtained by "Motor Cycle" staff at the Motor Industry Research Association's proving ground, Lindley, Leicestershire.)

MEAN MAXIMUM SPEED: 104 mph (14-stone rider wearing two-piece leathers).

HIGHEST ONE-WAY SPEED: 114 mph (strong tail wind).

BRAKING: From 30 mph to rest on dry tarmac, 28ft 6in.

TURNING CIRCLE: 19ft.

MINIMUM NON-SNATCH SPEED: 28 mph in top gear.

WEIGHT PER CC: 0.79 lb